Not For Resale
THIS IS A FREE BOOK

www.bookthing.org
THIS BOOK THING OF BALTIMORE, INC.

A Stroll in the Air
Frenzy For Two, Or More

Previously Published
Amédée, The New Tenant, Victims of Duty
The Bald Soprano
Exit the King
Fragments of a Journal
Four Plays
The Killer and Other Plays
Notes and Counter Notes
Rhinoceros and Other Plays

EUGÈNE IONESCO

A Stroll in the Air
Frenzy for Two,
Or More

Translated by Donald Watson

Grove Press, Inc.   New York

Copyright © 1965 by John Calder Ltd.
All Rights Reserved

A Stroll in the Air was originally published as *Le Piéton de l'Air* and *Frenzy for Two, Or More* as *Délire à Deux*, copyright © 1963 by Éditions Gallimard, Paris, France.

Library of Congress Catalog Card Number: 68-56364

Second Printing

Caution: This play is fully protected, in whole, in part or in any form under the copyright laws of the United States of America, the British Empire including the Dominion of Canada, and all other countries of the Copyright Union, and is subject to royalty. All rights, including professional, amateur, motion picture, radio, television, recitation, public reading, and any method of photographic reproduction, are strictly reserved. For professional rights all inquiries should be addressed to Grove Press, Inc., 80 University Place, New York, N.Y. For amateur rights all inquiries should be addressed to Samuel French, Inc., 25 West 45th Street, New York, N.Y.

DISTRIBUTED BY RANDOM HOUSE, INC., NEW YORK

Manufactured in the United States of America

CONTENTS

A STROLL IN THE AIR　　　　　　　　　　　7
FRENZY FOR TWO, OR MORE　　　　　　119

A Stroll in the Air

*To Madeleine Renaud
and Jean-Louis Barrault*

This play was first produced by Jean-Louis Barrault at the Odéon-Théâtre de France, on February 8, 1963. Set and costumes were by Jacques Noël, the music was by Georges Delerue and special effects were by Guy Bort.

CHARACTERS

MONSIEUR BÉRENGER, the Heavenly Hiker
MADAME BÉRENGER, his wife Joséphine
MLLE. BÉRENGER, his daughter Marthe
JOURNALIST (ENGLISH)
FIRST ENGLISHMAN, in his Sunday best (FIRST MAN)*
FIRST ENGLISHWOMAN, his wife (FIRST WOMAN)*
LITTLE BOY, their son
SECOND ENGLISHMAN, in his Sunday best (SECOND MAN)*
SECOND ENGLISHWOMAN, his wife (SECOND WOMAN)*
LITTLE GIRL, their daughter
JOHN BULL, chorus leader
FIRST OLD ENGLISH LADY (FIRST LADY)*
SECOND OLD ENGLISH LADY (SECOND LADY)*
DOCTOR-UNCLE
UNDERTAKER'S MAN (UNDERTAKER)*
VISITOR FROM THE ANTI-WORLD
Members of the Court of Justice:
    THE JUDGE
    AN ASSESSOR
    JOHN BULL, disguised as an executioner
THE MAN IN WHITE
    * Abbreviations used to designate the characters.

THE SET

On the extreme stage left a small house in the country, English style: a cottage, realized a little in the manner of Douanier Rousseau or perhaps Utrillo or even Chagall, according to the designer's taste. This little house, like the landscape described below, should have a dreamlike quality. In any case the dreamlike effect should be achieved rather by the methods used by a Primitive artist, consciously naive, than by those of a Surrealist artist, or one inspired by the technique of the Opéra or the Châtelet theater. Everything is fully lit, and so there should be nothing dim and no gauze, etc. . . .

The rest of the stage represents a grassy down, very green and very fresh, overlooking a valley; at the back of the stage you can see the hill opposite. The top of the downs where the action takes place should be semicircular and give the feeling that we are almost on the edge of a cliff that drops away into a gorge, allowing a glimpse in the background stage right of the outlying houses of a small English country town, very white and drenched in April sunshine. The sky is very blue and very pure. A few trees can be seen on the stage: cherry trees and pear trees in blossom.

The very faint sound of trains can be heard passing down in the gorge, alongside a small navigable river, which is also invisible, of course, but whose presence can be suggested by the distant sound of ships' hooters. You can see the cables of a telpher railway with two little red cabins going up and down.

Later, as the action advances, we shall see further props and changes in the setting. During the walk taken by BÉRENGER *and his family, for example, along the edge of the cliff, we shall see: pink ruins smothered in flowers, infinite space beyond the precipice, a silver bridge, a rack railway on the hillside, opposite, etc. . . .*

When the curtain rises two old ENGLISH LADIES *are taking a walk from stage right to stage left.*

FIRST LADY: Oh, yes.

SECOND LADY: Yes, we're in England.

FIRST LADY: In Gloucestershire.

SECOND LADY: What lovely weather for a Sunday.

Church bells are heard.

They're the bells from the Catholic church.

FIRST LADY: There was no Catholic church in my village.

At this moment the SECOND OLD LADY *is struck by a ball and turns around as a little* ENGLISH BOY *arrives on the stage.*

SECOND LADY: Oh!

FIRST LADY: (*to the* LITTLE BOY): Oh! You naughty little boy!

The FIRST ENGLISHMAN *appears, the father of the* LITTLE BOY.

FIRST MAN: So sorry, please excuse my little boy.

LITTLE BOY: I didn't do it on purpose.

16 / Eugène Ionesco

The FIRST ENGLISHWOMAN *arrives, the wife of the* FIRST ENGLISHMAN *and mother of the* LITTLE BOY.

FIRST WOMAN (*to the* LITTLE BOY): You must be more careful. That's no way to behave. Go and tell the lady you're sorry.

LITTLE BOY: I'm sorry.

FIRST MAN (*to the* LADIES): I'm really very sorry.

FIRST WOMAN (*to the* LADIES): I'm really very sorry.

The two OLD LADIES *and the parents greet one another, saying:* "Sorry, we're so sorry." *They separate, continuing their walk in opposite directions, while a* LITTLE ENGLISH GIRL *arrives, picks up the Little Boy's ball and gives it back to him.*

FIRST WOMAN (*to the* LITTLE GIRL): You've been very well brought up, little girl.

The LITTLE GIRL *bobs a curtsy and the* SECOND ENGLISHMAN *and his wife arrive, the parents of the* LITTLE GIRL.

FIRST WOMAN (*to the parents*): Your little girl is very well brought up.

FIRST MAN (*to the* SECOND MAN): Your little girl is very well brought up.

SECOND MAN (*to* FIRST MAN): And I'm sure your little boy must be too.

FIRST WOMAN: He's not as polite as all that.

SECOND WOMAN: Our little girl isn't always so polite either.

The two English couples greet each other in turns, say-

A Stroll in the Air / 17

ing: "So sorry, so sorry." *They turn away and continue their walk separately while the* FIRST WOMAN *delivers a parting shot at the* LITTLE BOY: *"You naughty boy"! The* LITTLE BOY *thumbs his nose at his parents on the sly.*

LITTLE GIRL: Oh! What a naughty little boy!

FIRST LADY (*who has seen what happened*): Oh! what a naughty little boy!

SECOND LADY: Oh! You naughty boy!

LITTLE GIRL: I won't say anything. It's not nice to tell tales.

Enter the JOURNALIST *from stage left, from behind Bérenger's house.*

JOURNALIST (*to* FIRST MAN): Aoh! Good morning!

FIRST WOMAN: Ooh! What a fine Sunday morning, isn't it!

FIRST MAN: What a fine Sunday morning!

JOURNALIST: It's just the weather to spend Sunday in the country.

The English people go out, quietly continuing their walk. All except the JOURNALIST, *who moves toward Bérenger's cottage. At this moment* BÉRENGER *puts his head through the window, looking at the sky and grass, and says:*

BÉRENGER: What a fine Sunday morning!

JOURNALIST: Oh please, Monsieur Bérenger. You are Monsieur Bérenger, aren't you? Excuse me, I'm a journalist . . .

BÉRENGER *makes as if to withdraw.*

18 / *Eugène Ionesco*

Please, don't go away.

Bérenger's head pops out again, in Punch and Judy style.

I only wanted to ask you a few questions.

Bérenger's head disappears.

Only some very simple questions. *Please,* Monsieur Bérenger. Just one question.

BÉRENGER *pops his head out again.*

BÉRENGER: I have decided, Monsieur, not to answer any more questions from newspapermen. (*His head disappears again.*)

JOURNALIST: Only one question. It's not a question from a newspaperman, it's a question from the newspaper. I've been sent here specially to ask you this question. It's nothing serious, nothing serious, don't worry.

BÉRENGER (*popping his head out again*): I haven't got much time, I've work to do. Or perhaps I haven't any yet, or perhaps I'll find some, who knows? I've come to England from the Continent to rest, to get away from work. . . .

JOURNALIST (*taking out his notebook*): Yes, we know. You've come to England, to Gloucestershire, and you live in a little prefabricated house, in the middle of this grassy field, right on top of the green downs overlooking the gorge, where there's a small navigable river (*While he is talking, the* JOURNALIST *points to the different parts of the set.*) flowing between two wooded hills. . . . We've already obtained this information,

Monsieur, forgive us for being so indiscreet. It was well meant.

BÉRENGER: It's not a secret. Besides, anyone can see.

JOURNALIST: My newspaper would like to ask you a question, dear Monsieur Bérenger.

BÉRENGER: I don't answer questions any more. (BÉRENGER *makes as if to withdraw. His head disappears and reappears.*)

JOURNALIST: Don't go away, Monsieur Bérenger. It's a very simple question. You can answer how you like. It's to put on the front page, with a big photograph of you half life-size.

BÉRENGER: Well, be quick about it. I haven't got much time. I'm having a rest.

JOURNALIST: Forgive me, I'm very sorry to disturb you. I'm going to ask you the traditional question: when shall we see in the great theaters of the world one of your new masterpieces?

BÉRENGER: I don't want to answer that question.

JOURNALIST: Oh, yes, please, Monsieur Bérenger.

BÉRENGER: I shall have to make you a confession. I've always known I never had any reason to write.

JOURNALIST: That's perfectly understandable. But that's not a reason to have no reason to write. There's no reason for anything, we all know that.

BÉRENGER: Of course we do. But people still do things though there's no reason for doing them. Anyway, the weaker brethren invent apparent reasons for their actions. They pretend to believe in them. We can't avoid doing something, they say. I'm not one of *them*. Once upon a time, though I'm really a nihilist, there was some strange force inside me that made me do things and made me write. I can't go on any longer.

JOURNALIST: I'll jot that down. You can't go on any longer.

BÉRENGER: No, I can't. For years it was a consolation to me to be able to say there was nothing to say. But now I feel far too sure I was right. I'm convinced of it. But not intellectually or psychologically. Now it's a deeply held conviction, it's got into my flesh and blood and bones, it's physiological. It paralyzes me. Writing isn't a game for me any more, and it will never be a game again. It ought to lead to something else, but it doesn't.

JOURNALIST: What should it lead to?

BÉRENGER: If I knew that, there'd be no problem.

JOURNALIST: Give us a message.

BÉRENGER: They've all been given before. You've got them all to hand, as many as you want. The cafés and the newspaper offices are swarming with literary geniuses who have solved everything. Really in the know. There's nothing easier than a mechanical message. Luckily for them. They believe in the straight and narrow path of Historical Necessity, but History is really round the bend. For them, might is right, so Historical Necessity is the doctrine of the victorious party in power, whatever it may be, they believe that History is right. You can always find the best of reasons to justify a victorious ideology. But it's just when it's victorious and comes to power, that it starts going wrong. You need discrimination, intellectual courage or penetrating insight if you're going to be able to resist what's with us now and foresee what will be, or even just feel that there ought to be something different.

JOURNALIST: Some people say it's really because you're afraid of rivals that you may be temporarily giving up the theater.

BÉRENGER: I think it's rather because I need renovating inside. Shall I be able to renovate myself? In theory, yes, in theory, I will, because I don't approve of the way things are going. The few people who disapprove of the way things are going are the only ones who can say anything new. The truth is to be found in a kind of neurosis. . . . It's not there in a healthy mind, in neurosis lies the truth, tomorrow's truth, which contradicts the apparent truth of today. All writers, or almost all, and almost all the playwrights are denouncing yesterday's evils, injustices, alienations, yesterday's diseases. They close their eyes to the evils of today. But it's no use denouncing an old evil. It's pointless to demystify what has been demystified already. That's just being conformist. All that it does is conceal the new disease, the new injustices, the new deceptions. Most contemporary writers think they're an advance guard, that History has really left them far behind. They are stupid, they're not courageous at all.

JOURNALIST: One moment, please. . . . So your plays *are* plays with a message? Not like anybody else's message, but a message all the same. . . . Your message . . .

BÉRENGER: I'm afraid it's against my principles, but I hope

there's something else behind my apparent message, I still don't quite know what, but perhaps it will reveal itself . . . as the play goes on . . . through my imagination . . .

JOURNALIST: Let me take this down: down with the way things are . . . neurosis . . . cafés . . . discrimination . . . courage, intuition . . . diseases . . . writers are stupid.

BÉRENGER: And then, good or bad, the critics make me tired. And then the theater makes me tired, and actors make me tired; and life makes me tired.

JOURNALIST: Got that: tired . . . tired . . . tired. . . .

BÉRENGER: Sometimes too I wonder whether literature and the theater can ever give a full account of reality, it's so complex, so overwhelming. And I wonder if, nowadays, anyone can get a clear image of other people or of himself. We are living a horrible nightmare. Literature has never been so powerful, so vivid, or so intense as life. And certainly not today. If it wants to be compared with life, literature ought to be a thousand times more cruel and terrifying than it is. However cruel it becomes, literature can only give a very dim and feeble picture of how cruel life is in reality; or how marvelous it can be too. Literature isn't knowledge either, as it's nothing but a cliché: I mean, it gets stereotyped, at once it becomes hidebound, set in its expression, which lags behind instead of leading the way. What must we do to make literature an exciting voyage of discovery? Even imagination is not enough. Orthodox men of letters—and all men of letters are orthodox—believe they know or reflect reality. But reality surpasses fiction; it cannot be grasped any more, even by the conscious mind. . . .

JOURNALIST: I now put on record that it can no longer be recorded.

BÉRENGER: But I suppose we could put up with anything providing we were immortal. I am paralyzed by the knowledge that I'm going to die. There's nothing new about that truth. But it's a truth we forget . . . so that we can *do* something. I don't want to *do* anything any more, I want to be cured of death. *Au revoir,* Monsieur.

JOURNALIST: That's fine. Thank you for that enlightening statement. I'm sure it will be of lively interest to our Sunday readers. Give them something really entertaining. I'd like to offer you a special vote of thanks, for giving me something that will help to fill up my column.

BÉRENGER: Front page, with the photograph, please.

JOURNALIST: Of course, Monsieur. You'll receive the check tomorrow.

BÉRENGER: How much?

The JOURNALIST *cups his hands and mentions an inaudible figure to* BÉRENGER.

Right, that'll do, Monsieur. *Au revoir,* Monsieur.

Bérenger's head disappears. The JOURNALIST *goes off stage right. The stage is empty for a few moments. In the distance you can hear the throbbing of a plane which will go on increasing in volume during the following scene.* MME. BÉRENGER—JOSÉPHINE—*dressed in a dark blue peignoir with a white star-shaped pattern, comes in from the right. Behind her comes the* DOCTOR-UNCLE, *followed in turn by the* UNDERTAKER'S

MAN. *The latter is wearing a black suit, black gloves and a black tie and carrying a black bowler hat. The* DOCTOR-UNCLE *is graying at the temples, he wears a gray suit with black crape on the lapel of the jacket.*

DOCTOR-UNCLE (*catching* JOSÉPHINE *up*): Joséphine! Joséphine!

JOSÉPHINE (*turning around*): It's you, Doctor-Uncle? I thought you were in Brazzaville....

DOCTOR-UNCLE: I've never been to Brazzaville.

UNDERTAKER: Madame Bérenger, Madame Bérenger....

JOSÉPHINE: What is it, Monsieur?

UNDERTAKER: Excuse me, Madame Bérenger, allow me to introduce myself: I'm the undertaker's man. I've some rather distressing news for you.

JOSÉPHINE: Oh! Heavens!

DOCTOR-UNCLE: It's not distressing news at all, don't worry, little Joséphine. On the contrary, it's very pleasant news.

UNDERTAKER: That depends on your point of view. Perhaps it is pleasant news, but it's distressing enough for us.

JOSÉPHINE: But what on earth has happened?

UNDERTAKER: Have no fear, Madame, it's quite terrible.

DOCTOR-UNCLE (*to the* UNDERTAKER): Let me break the news to my niece myself. I must be careful how I tell her. People can die of great joy and great sorrow. (*To* JOSÉPHINE:) My brother, your father . . .

JOSÉPHINE: I know, the poor man died in the war. They brought his body back.

DOCTOR-UNCLE: He's not dead any more, Joséphine.

JOSÉPHINE: Raised from the dead? Stop joking, Uncle.

DOCTOR-UNCLE: I don't know whether he's been raised from the dead, but he's alive all right, take my word as a doctor. Perhaps we've only believed he was dead. We were wrong. In any case he's not far off, he'll be here any moment now.

JOSÉPHINE: It's impossible, impossible!

DOCTOR-UNCLE: I swear it's true!

JOSÉPHINE: How is he? Where is he? Has he lost weight? Is he tired? Is he ill? Is he sad? Is he happy?

UNDERTAKER: But what about us, Madame, what are *we* going to do? You've announced this gentleman's, your father's decease officially, you've ordered an interment. Everything's ready, we've announced it in the newspapers, we've paid out all the expenses.

JOSÉPHINE: Oh! My poor father! It's so long since I saw him. Do you think I'll recognize him?

DOCTOR-UNCLE: He's younger than before his death was announced. He looks as he did in that old photo taken before he went off to the war. He's lost weight, yes of course. He is pale. He has long hair. He's been wounded.

JOSÉPHINE: Father, where are you? I can't wait any longer, I want to see him at once.

UNDERTAKER: Don't be in such a hurry, Madame. You

must regularize the situation first. This is very prejudicial to our financial and moral interests. The excellent reputation of our firm, founded in 1784, five years before your French Revolution . . .

DOCTOR-UNCLE: We must cancel the interment. . . .

UNDERTAKER: And here I am, left with a funeral on my hands!

DOCTOR-UNCLE: It won't be wasted. There's quite a demand.

JOSÉPHINE: Oh yes, of course, we must cancel it.

DOCTOR-UNCLE: We'll pay you for everything.

UNDERTAKER: That's not good enough, sir.

DOCTOR-UNCLE: What's more, we offer you our apologies.

UNDERTAKER: I accept them, sir, but there's more than that at stake. We've sent in a public obituary notice, we've advertised it, and now the burial won't take place. Who will have confidence in us again?

JOSÉPHINE: All right, take us to court and we'll pay you all the necessary damages.

UNDERTAKER: There's never been a case like this before. We'll take it to the Chamber of Commerce. And then to the Court of Appeal. We'll make a precedent of it. I protest, I protest most vigorously. I'll have my lawyer on you, with the judge and all the ushers.

JOSÉPHINE: Oh, Monsieur, don't get so angry. You're not going to upset my poor father again.

UNDERTAKER (*going off*): You'll hear more of this, you

A Stroll in the Air / 27

won't get away with it. I'll make a scandal and it'll get in all the papers. (*He goes out.*)

DOCTOR-UNCLE: We'll see our lawyer about it, don't worry, it'll be all right. Even if the papers do mention it, we can always say it was a miracle. And that our intentions were honorable.

JOSÉPHINE: We shouldn't have announced the funeral so quickly.... Now we've got to start sending out resurrection cards, resurrection cards! But where is he?

DOCTOR-UNCLE (*pointing into space*): Here, he's over there.

JOSÉPHINE: Father, I want to kiss you, show yourself. I can't see him, I can't see you, where are you?

DOCTOR-UNCLE (*still pointing into space*): Over there, look, he's over there!

JOSÉPHINE: Show yourself, Father, show yourself. It doesn't matter if the undertakers are angry, that doesn't matter. Show yourself.

The noise of the plane has become deafening. It is so loud that it doubtless drowns the inaudible dialogue between JOSÉPHINE *and the* DOCTOR-UNCLE, *which probably follows. For a few moments these two characters go on acting wordlessly in the uproar.*

The stage has been getting darker as the noise increased in volume, and now it is in darkness. Suddenly a bomb is heard exploding on Bérenger's cottage, which for a couple of seconds we can see lit up in the flash of the explosion and even in flames, if possible.

Utter darkness again, for a few very brief moments and

the throbbing of the plane gradually dying away. After the next four or five lines of dialogue that come, it will be heard no more.

Lights. Bérenger's cottage is a pile of smoking ruins. BÉRENGER *is seen framed in the doorway, which alone has remained intact.*

JOSÉPHINE *is standing on the right, dressed in a sky-blue suit of rather classical cut, with a rose pinned on the lapel, carrying a black leather handbag. On her head, a little pink hat.*

Next to JOSÉPHINE *is* MLLE. BÉRENGER, *whose Christian name is* MARTHE. *She is wearing a pink Sunday dress, white shoes, a little white embroidered collar around the neck, and she is carrying a small white handbag. She has long chestnut hair, gentle gray-green eyes, and a good clear profile, if rather severe. She is wearing white stockings.*

The English characters are at the back of the stage, with their back to the public.

Each of the two OLD LADIES *is right at one side of the stage. Nearer the center of the stage, at the back, are the First and Second Couples, with their Children. The* LITTLE BOY *and the* LITTLE GIRL *are both holding a croquet mallet. All the English characters are quite still, looking up at the sky as if they were following the airplane out of sight. At the back of the stage, dead center, stands* JOHN BULL *in his characteristic and well-known costume.* JOHN BULL *is the only English character not to be watching the plane. You can see him, like an enormous puppet, slowly taking off his typical hat to wipe the sweat from the inside. Then he mops his brow with a large handkerchief, and puts the handkerchief back in his pocket and the hat back on his head, while he slowly turns to face the public. Once this movement has been accomplished, he stands with his legs wide apart and his arms behind his back.*

In their corner of the stage MME. *and* MLLE. BÉRENGER *are not watching the plane either. They are talking.*

MARTHE: *Ma petite Maman,* you're all upset. I wish I could dream of Grandpa, just to know what he was like. I wish I could meet him.

JOSÉPHINE: I'd forgotten I missed him so much. Now I remember how it hurt to see him go.

MARTHE: We've got Papa now.

BÉRENGER (*looking at the sky, to the English*): It's a German bomber. Left over from the last war.

The English characters turn around all together.

FIRST WOMAN (*showing her* LITTLE GIRL *to the other English people*): She wants to be a prima donna.

JOSÉPHINE: Of course, but I'm afraid no one's replaceable. When someone's disappeared, it leaves a gap you can never quite fill.

BÉRENGER (*to the English*): It's a good thing I was in the doorway. I wanted to walk about in the fresh grass, under your blue sky, as beautiful as the sky in June, a beautiful English blue.

JOHN BULL (*to the* LITTLE BOY): And what do *you* want to be?

LITTLE BOY: A pilot.

30 / *Eugène Ionesco*

SECOND MAN (*to* BÉRENGER): Oh yes, Spring's a lovely season here.

SECOND LADY: It doesn't rain so much.

JOHN BULL (*to* LITTLE BOY): And why a pilot, my child?

MARTHE (*to* JOSÉPHINE): Better not say a word to Papa, perhaps, about your dream.

LITTLE BOY (*to* JOHN BULL): To drop bombs on the houses.

FIRST LADY (*to* FIRST WOMAN): Let her sing us something.

JOHN BULL (*to the* LITTLE GIRL): Sing us a nice song, my child.

LITTLE GIRL: No!

ALL THE ENGLISH (*together*): Sing us something.

MARTHE (*to* JOSÉPHINE): Oh! Look at the countryside . . . the valley . . . Look at those little English children.

THE ENGLISH (*to the* LITTLE GIRL): Sing us a nice song.

MARTHE (*to* JOSÉPHINE): Look, there's Papa, he's seen us.

BÉRENGER *advances toward* JOSÉPHINE *and* MARTHE.

Papa! Isn't this a lovely field!

SECOND LADY (*pointing to* JOHN BULL): If you won't sing us a song, that man will eat you up.

BÉRENGER (*to his wife*): Did you see what's just happened to me?

FIRST COUPLE (*to* LITTLE GIRL): Sing, little girl!

JOSÉPHINE (*to* BÉRENGER): What did I tell you? You ought to be more careful.

SECOND COUPLE: Sing, little daughter!

BÉRENGER: It's not *my* fault. I wasn't in the plane. How could I help it?

THE TWO LADIES: Sing, young Miss!

JOSÉPHINE: You ought to have bought a more solid house, not a cardboard shack like that, which collapses at the slightest bomb. It's made an awful mess of your notebooks.

MARTHE: Leave him alone, *Maman.* (*To* BÉRENGER:) We had a lovely journey down from London. It was all so green, and there were rivers and little towns like toy models and red and yellow cars on the roads. Was it nice and quiet for you to work?

BÉRENGER: Yes. If it hadn't been for the plane.

JOSÉPHINE: You couldn't have found a better excuse for not working.

The LITTLE GIRL *suddenly starts singing. In fact, all she produces is a series of trills, just like a little mechanical nightingale.*

MARTHE: Oh! It's the little English girl singing. (*Fresh trills.*) Doesn't she sing nicely? I wish I could sing like that.

JOHN BULL (*to the* LITTLE GIRL): Oh, that's very pretty.

SECOND WOMAN: It's an old song from our part of the country.

FIRST LADY: My Grandfather used to sing me that.

FIRST MAN: My Grandfather used to sing it to me too.

JOHN BULL: It's known everywhere in England. But with us it was a little different. We used to sing it like this. *He sings. Again, like the trills of a mechanical nightingale, exactly the same as before.*

Then all the English sing the same trills in chorus. Only John Bull's voice comes through a little lower and the Little Girl's voice a little higher.

This musical sequence must be very short.

The production should not insist on this scene, or complicate it. The English characters must just have enough time to smile a couple of times while they sing. In fact, they will only open their mouths, as a mechanical nightingale will be hidden somewhere to sing for them.

The LITTLE BOY *pulls the Little Girl's pigtails and she appears quite bald.*

THE BÉRENGER FAMILY: Oh!

SECOND WOMAN: Well, yes, our little girl is the little bald prima donna.

None of the English characters or the BÉRENGER FAMILY *are the slightest bit surprised by this and it passes off quite naturally. All that happens is that the Little Boy's mother snatches the Little Girl's wig and gives it to her Father who hands it over to her Mother who passes it back to her.*

The Little Boy's Father smacks his son on the hand and signs to him to go up to the LITTLE GIRL. *The* LITTLE BOY *goes and kisses the* LITTLE GIRL, *then the two English children go and play croquet in the left-hand corner of the stage, from which they will disappear into the wings.*

JOHN BULL *has a few words with the two couples in turn, then with the* OLD LADIES, *and slowly, one after the other, they all pass into the wings; later they will appear again in groups, cross the stage and disappear again, sometimes a few of them, sometimes a larger number, in order to provide a kind of moving background. All these directions apply to the moves of these characters during the following scene. The English characters will appear together again only when they are wanted, and this will be indicated.*

MARTHE (*conversing, therefore, with* JOSÉPHINE *and* BÉRENGER, *against a background of English people walking slowly about, to emphasize the gentle country atmosphere*): Look at *Maman's* pretty hat!

BÉRENGER (*to* JOSÉPHINE): It suits you very well, *chérie*, and tones with your sky-blue costume.

MARTHE: *Maman's* little tailor-made is quite classical. The classical cut suits her very well. Doesn't she look sweet in it? Look, Papa, have you noticed? She's got a rose pinned to the lapel, a red rose. Do you see?

BÉRENGER: I'm not so absent-minded as you all think.

JOSÉPHINE: If Marthe hadn't drawn your attention to it you'd never have noticed.

MARTHE: Oh, *Maman*, please! (*Then to* BÉRENGER:) The colors go very well together. She's got very good taste, *Maman*.

BÉRENGER: Indeed she has. It's all very nice. Except for the black leather handbag, which doesn't quite go with the rest.

JOSÉPHINE: I can't buy everything all at once, you know quite well. It's too expensive.

MARTHE: We saw a lovely bag for *Maman* in the window of a shop in Piccadilly, a light color, I'm not quite sure what shade, with flowers on it that moved and closed and opened and closed again, like real flowers, you'd really think they *were* flowers.

BÉRENGER: Perhaps they were real flowers. . . .

MARTHE: Yes, perhaps real flowers or perhaps little hands like fans. It was so pretty. I don't know why but it makes me feel happy, a thing like that. I did so want that bag for *Maman*. You'll give it to her as a present, won't you? For her birthday?

BÉRENGER: Tomorrow, if she likes.

JOSÉPHINE: There's no hurry. For my birthday, if you like. We mustn't spend everything all at once. I'll make do with this one for now: we've got your house to build again. Where are you going to work now?

BÉRENGER: Don't worry about that. There's no shortage of houses, you find them in all the towns, all the villages, along all the roads and even in the depths of the country. And even on the water. Nothing but houses. And to think there are people who complain they don't know where to live.

JOSÉPHINE: There are more people than houses.

BÉRENGER: Not in the countryside.

JOSÉPHINE: Oh, you can't count.

MARTHE: All the people could take it in turns to use them.

BÉRENGER: Don't worry about your dream. It's only a dream, that's all.

JOSÉPHINE: You really think so?

BÉRENGER: Why yes, why yes, I'm sure it was.

MARTHE (*to* JOSÉPHINE): You shouldn't have told him about it.

JOSÉPHINE (*to* BÉRENGER): I can't help it upsetting me. It was my father.

BÉRENGER: Of course I understand. But that only means you were very fond of your father, that you very much wish he was still alive and that you realize it's not possible, it's just not possible. It's when we dream about our loved ones that we really notice how much we miss them, how very much we miss them.

JOSÉPHINE: That's exactly what I was saying just now.

BÉRENGER: In the daytime we forget. We don't think about it. If we were as sharply conscious of things all the time as we are in our dreams, we couldn't go on living. It's at night we remember. The daytime is made for forgetting. Don't let your dream upset you, just have a look at this grass. . . .

MARTHE: Don't cry, *Maman*. Papa's right.

BÉRENGER: Look at the grass, and look at those woods opposite, on the other side of the gorge. Enjoy it all. Turn around. . . .

MARTHE (*to* JOSÉPHINE): Turn around. . . .

JOSÉPHINE (*turning around*): All right, all right, I can turn around on my own. . . .

BÉRENGER: Better look at those white walls of the first houses in the town. . . .

MARTHE: They look as if they're going to melt in the light.

JOSÉPHINE: It's very pretty.

MARTHE: It's more than pretty.

BÉRENGER: Look at the sky!

MARTHE: Look at it!

JOSÉPHINE: But I *am* looking, what else do you want?

BÉRENGER: Look, look at it! Let the light be enough to make you happy. Have you ever seen anything so gentle, so pure and fresh?

JOSÉPHINE: Yes, I'm still thinking of . . .

MARTHE: Stop thinking, *Maman,* stop thinking. Enjoy yourself!

JOSÉPHINE: I'll enjoy myself, if you like.

BÉRENGER: There's a very beautiful view from the edge of the gorge. I'll take you both by the hand and we'll go for a lovely walk.

MARTHE (*giving her hand to* BÉRENGER; *and to* JOSÉPHINE): Give him your hand.

BÉRENGER (*to* JOSÉPHINE): Come on, hand in hand, and you'll forget your worries.

JOSÉPHINE *gives her hand hesitantly to* BÉRENGER, *or rather it is* BÉRENGER *who takes hers in his.*

JOSÉPHINE: There's so much waiting to be done at home. The pancakes and the salad for the week...

MARTHE: Come on, *Maman,* it's Sunday. Sunday is a day of rest.

The English characters now come on the stage from the left, one by one or in pairs, as is indicated subsequently, and go out on the right. They can return in the opposite direction if necessary.

Meanwhile a curtain or screen, with the various items to be mentioned, will move in the same direction as the English characters are walking. The BÉRENGER FAMILY *will walk in the opposite direction to the screen at the back, or rather will pretend to be walking.*

At the front of the stage the two children playing croquet will move in the opposite direction to the English parents. They will leave the stage and then come back. Or perhaps they can just move from the one side of the stage to the other and then back again in the opposite direction up to the moment when they finally disappear.

FIRST LADY (*appearing with the* SECOND LADY): I felt like a prisoner in this country and there was no escape. I'd been living there quite a long time. I was so frightened I never really wanted to leave it, but when I found out I wasn't allowed to leave it, I was even more frightened. I could see nothing but walls all around me. Walls everywhere. I had a nervous breakdown. Claustrophobia. It's not being unable to leave that's so bad, it's *knowing* that you *can't.*

SECOND LADY: I quite understand, my dear.

38 / *Eugène Ionesco*

The two OLD LADIES *go out.*

BÉRENGER, JOSÉPHINE *and* MARTHE *go to the right-hand side of the stage and start walking at the back from right to left. You can hear the distant sound of a train and the whistle from the engine. A tiny little train can be seen in the distance, with red carriages.*

MARTHE: Oh, look, Papa, look, *Maman,* what a pretty little train! It's like a toy one.

BÉRENGER: Joséphine, look, you'd think it *was* a toy....

They can stop walking for a moment and have a good look around them before continuing their stroll.

FIRST MAN (*appearing with the* SECOND MAN): I've wasted my whole life, trying to make up my mind to change it. When I lay awake at night, I used to say to myself: "Tomorrow I'll break with everything and I *will* change."

SECOND MAN: Change what?

FIRST MAN: Life, *my* life, the life *I've* been leading is someone else's life.

SECOND MAN: And did you keep your promise?

BÉRENGER: That's the kind of train I should like to have had when I was a child. But I'm afraid the children of today don't want them any more, all they like is rockets. And a train like that is just a museum piece—all right for archaeologists. No one can understand it any more without a lot of phony historical reconstruction.

MARTHE: I'd like to have a doll, too, that walks all by itself, makes wee-wee and talks.

A Stroll in the Air / 39

JOSÉPHINE: You're too big to play with dolls now. Did you finish your homework for tomorrow?

SECOND MAN: Did you keep your promise?

FIRST MAN: I did when I first woke up in the morning.... But after breakfast I felt much too heavy. I put it off to the next day. And so on for years and years and years and years.

SECOND MAN: You oughtn't to have had any breakfast.

FIRST MAN: Now it's too late. But I'm still trying. How many breakfasts do you have in thirty years?

SECOND MAN: Easy enough to calculate.

They go out.

BÉRENGER: What's the good of regretting what might have been? What's the good of it?

JOSÉPHINE: We all have our regrets. But they don't do us any good.

MARTHE: *Maman's* quite right, it doesn't do us any good regretting the past.

BÉRENGER: Yes, that's true. Especially when it's a lovely day like today.

FIRST WOMAN (*appearing with the* SECOND WOMAN): How can I describe it to you? That town was so sad and ugly. You know what I mean?

SECOND WOMAN: Nothing surprising about that.

FIRST WOMAN: Quite by chance I found this street. A beautiful street it was, so beautiful I could have wept. In all that ghastly town, just one beautiful street, empty and beautiful, and no one knew about it. You believe me, don't you? And right at the end, a castle keep. Heavens, how beautiful it was. Indescribably beautiful. How can I tell you, how can I tell you . . .

SECOND WOMAN: Don't say a word.

FIRST WOMAN: When it's too beautiful, it's heartbreaking.

Enter JOHN BULL.

BÉRENGER: It's the river that starts somewhere near Bath. You see, it's making for the Ocean. (*Pointing.*) The sea is in that direction, and the port. . . . It's a port bigger than Liverpool, but there's nothing gloomy about it. It's the only English city with colors like the Mediterranean. Look down there, the ships are taking their merchandise.

Melodious sounds are heard, voices or something resembling voices singing.

Listen!

JOHN BULL: It appears we should pay great attention to what the poets say. They are often right. That's what I've been told. They prophesy and their prophecies come true. I prefer sausages. I'd rather have my dog. (JOHN BULL *goes off.*)

JOSÉPHINE: I can't hear anything.

Enter the JOURNALIST.

MARTHE: Why yes, listen. . . .

JOURNALIST: I ought to give it up. (*He stops and faces the public.*) I ought to give it up. After all, up to what age can you go on being interested in art? Art and

A Stroll in the Air / 41

literature, that's kid's stuff. Art has lost its power; if it ever had any. (*The* JOURNALIST *goes off.*)

JOSÉPHINE: Why yes! What *is* that music? Those lovely voices?

BÉRENGER: They're sirens' voices from the ships.

JOSÉPHINE: Ships' sirens, yes. But it's the sailors who start them up.

They continue their walk and see on the opposite side a fantastic turreted palace in the middle of the woods, and fields with motionless grazing cows; a train with different-colored carriages going up the rack railway; the screen at the back goes on moving and on the hill-top opposite you can see a little Eiffel Tower, a red balloon floating away, a blue lake and a waterfall, the terminus of a telpher railway, and a little rocket in a shower of sparks, etc. . . . and then woods again and trees in blossom.

The three BÉRENGERS *make no comment as they watch the scenery and the props, just a few exclamations: "Oh! Ah! Look, isn't it beautiful!"*

Meanwhile, walking in the opposite direction without looking at the landscape, the English characters are talking to one another.

FIRST WOMAN: It was black, black, black. You can't imagine how black it was. Black as snow in London. I'm not the author of that expression.

SECOND WOMAN: Sometimes I dreamt too, that I was walking about in a dreamlike city. All alone, absolutely alone.

42 / *Eugène Ionesco*

The two WOMEN *go out. Enter the* JOURNALIST *and* JOHN BULL.

MARTHE: Oh! Isn't it wonderful!

JOURNALIST: There's the contemplative man: the man who wants to be in harmony with the world. And the man of action: that's the man who wants to bring the world into harmony with himself. Which is the right solution?

JOHN BULL: He and the world must each play his part. Each go a part of the way to meet the other.

They both go out.

JOSÉPHINE: It's marvelous.

FIRST MAN (*reappearing with the* SECOND MAN): In the old days it took a long time to go to those little islands! The road to the Isles! The voyage lasted weeks. You gradually got used to all the different climates. They spoke unfamiliar languages and had surprising faces. And how long it used to take, even by rail! There was some space in the world in those days, plenty of it.

SECOND MAN: Now we have to look for it somewhere else.

They both go out.

BÉRENGER: Oh!

FIRST LADY (*reappearing with the* SECOND LADY): And the faces all look the same. Just like geese.

SECOND LADY: And it seems you never *feel* any older. You have to rely on other people *telling* you. You're always just there, at the center of things, you look all around you but you don't know. And when it happens, someone else has to tell you. I want to *know*.

A Stroll in the Air / 43

FIRST LADY: You have to get used to dying. It's more decent that way. You must be polite when you go. You must have time to say your good-bys. Without too many tears.

JOSÉPHINE (*looking through her lorgnette*): Oh!

SECOND LADY: My dear, it seems it's terribly easy. You get used to it so quickly. It's really quite amazing. You can give up everything straightaway, all at once, just like that.

THE BÉRENGER FAMILY (together): Oh! Oh! Oh! Look, isn't it beautiful!

FIRST LADY: It's incredible. Do you think it's true?

JOSÉPHINE (*looking at the countryside*): It's incredible.

SECOND LADY: I'm sure it is, it's very easy. You only have to close your eyes. And everything slips gently away.

BÉRENGER (*looking at the countryside*): Oh!

MARTHE (*looking at the countryside*): Oh! Ah!

FIRST LADY: No, *I* can't get used to it. Perhaps you're right, perhaps. . . . But I can't get used to it. I suppose the time hasn't come for me yet, I'll get used to it later on. When I'm old.

They both go out.

JOSÉPHINE (*stopping and still looking through her lorgnette*): I must say it's really very pretty.

All the English people who had gone out return, half from the left and half from the right of the stage. Among them, at first hidden by the others, on the left, is the VISITOR FROM THE ANTI-WORLD, *dressed in the old style, with white side whiskers.*

44 / Eugène Ionesco

Meanwhile a bench appears on the right and the BÉRENGER FAMILY *go and sit down facing the public, with* BÉRENGER *in the middle, all with their hands on their knees like a provincial family photograph at the beginning of the century.*

The English people meet in the center of the stage and they exchange greetings. The children follow their parents out. Those who pass the bench as they go off greet the BÉRENGER FAMILY.

Now only the BÉRENGER FAMILY *is on stage, with the* VISITOR FROM THE ANTI-WORLD, *whom no one has noticed.* THE VISITOR *moves slowly toward the bench, with a pipe upside down in his mouth.*

MARTHE: Look, that gentleman's different from the others.

JOSÉPHINE: What gentleman?

MARTHE: That gentleman all by himself.

BÉRENGER: So he is. (*While* THE VISITOR *quietly draws nearer.*) He's dressed in the old style.

JOSÉPHINE: But what gentleman are you talking about?

MARTHE: That old gentleman with white side whiskers.

BÉRENGER: Yes, he has got white side whiskers.

THE VISITOR *is quite near the* BÉRENGERS, *he approaches them without appearing to have noticed them and brushes so close to them that all except* JOSÉPHINE *draw back to make room and move their feet under the bench.*

BÉRENGER: Look out!

MARTHE: He's not a very polite man, is he? He might have

said he was sorry. English people are usually more polite.

Still walking at the same pace and without appearing to have noticed the BÉRENGER FAMILY, THE VISITOR *returns to the side of the stage he came from.*

JOSÉPHINE: But who is this gentleman you're talking about? You must be seeing things.

MARTHE: No, we're not. Didn't you see him with his pipe upside down? And the smoke going down instead of up?

BÉRENGER: Ah yes! I know.

THE VISITOR *goes toward the back of the stage and suddenly disappears above the valley.*

MARTHE: He's melted into thin air.

JOSÉPHINE: There you are! You really are seeing things.

BÉRENGER: Yes and no, yes and no.

MARTHE: Perhaps he fell over?

The three BÉRENGERS *have already come to their feet and moved a few paces toward* THE VISITOR *before he disappears.*

BÉRENGER: He didn't melt into the air and he didn't fall over. You can say he "fell" from the blue, if you like. He's going on with his walk, but we can't follow him any more. He's not a creature of this world. Although he moves among us, he's not one of us. He's from the Anti-World; he's gone right through the wall.

JOSÉPHINE: What wall?

BÉRENGER: Through the invisible wall. It's invisible, but we can't see through it.

> THE VISITOR FROM THE ANTI-WORLD *appears again for a brief moment above the gorge. He puts his hands behind his back and then disappears again.*

MARTHE: There he is again! Look!

BÉRENGER: Did you see him this time?

JOSÉPHINE: You'll send me out of my mind, the two of you.

MARTHE: He's disappeared again!

BÉRENGER: He's passed the frontier. He's gone home.

JOSÉPHINE: Where's his home, then? And who do you mean?

BÉRENGER: The gentleman from the Anti-World. He's gone back to his own world, the Anti-World. I see him sometimes in the mornings, he must take a walk every day at the same time and I suppose he goes past some place where there's a crack in the Anti-World, a kind of gap or no man's land between two worlds. (*To* MARTHE:) Now you understand why he can't see us and that's why he didn't say sorry when he passed in front of us.

JOSÉPHINE: Anyway, we can't take him at all seriously. Even if he really did exist he'd never be a useful person to know.

MARTHE: Papa, what is the Anti-World?

BÉRENGER: The Anti-World, the Anti-World, how can I explain it? There's no proof that it exists, but when you think about it, you can find it in your own thoughts. The evidence is in your mind. There's not just one Anti-World. There are several universes, and they're all interlocking.

MARTHE: How many are there?

BÉRENGER: There are numbers and numbers of them. An unknown quantity of numbers. These worlds interlink and interlock, without touching one another, for they can all coexist in the same space.

JOSÉPHINE: How's that?

BÉRENGER: I know it's difficult to imagine. But that's how it is.

MARTHE: That's what he says, so that's how it is.

JOSÉPHINE: Well how can you see an inhabitant of one of these worlds?

BÉRENGER: It is, indeed, a very exceptional case, I know it must be due to some error of adjustment.

MARTHE: Anyone in the world can make an error of adjustment.... In any world.

The FIRST WOMAN *enters from the right.*

JOSÉPHINE: It's just not good enough. Isn't there any other proof?

BÉRENGER: But I tell you the proof lies in our own minds, in what we discover when we think.

MARTHE: We discover them when we think, we think these universes, that's what he says, don't you hear?

FIRST WOMAN: You're looking for proof, aren't you? Forgive me interfering in your conversation. I thought I could help you. There is visual proof, you know.

JOSÉPHINE: Thank you.

FIRST WOMAN: In Ireland and in Scotland, I myself have seen in mirrors the outline of a landscape that is not of our world.

MARTHE: Is that really true?

BÉRENGER: You see?

JOSÉPHINE: And what's it like, this landscape? Could you describe it to us?

FIRST WOMAN: It is indescribable.

JOSÉPHINE: You should have brought one of these mirrors along with you.

FIRST WOMAN: What good would that do? The images can only be reflected because of a certain quality in the air of Ireland, or in the water of Scotland. If one looks in these mirrors anywhere else but Ireland or Scotland, this strange phenomenon never occurs.

JOSÉPHINE: It's very peculiar. But I suppose you're right. And yet these disappearances, and these appearances that disappear again. . . .

BÉRENGER: If we want a more detailed explanation, we shall have to ask a scientist. It's all quite beyond me.

The FIRST MAN *enters from the left.*

FIRST WOMAN: Here's my husband. (*To her husband*:) Show them your little mirror from Ireland.

The FIRST MAN *takes a mirror from his pocket. The other characters look at him, standing two or three paces away.*

JOSÉPHINE: I can't see anything.

BÉRENGER: Of course you can't see anything. That just proves you've got to go to Ireland to see this indescribable landscape in the mirrors. So it also proves that it can be proved.

MARTHE: Of course it does, it's the proof you were asking for.

The FIRST MAN *and his wife go up on the left, calling their little boy.*

FIRST WOMAN: Tony, be a good boy. Stop pulling the little soprano's hair!

FIRST MAN: If you don't, I'll pull your ears.

They go out. The BÉRENGER FAMILY *go on with their walk. They walk very slowly; it is the screen at the back that is moving. At exactly the same moment as the English people go out, there appears, on the opposite side of the stage, the profile, the pipe and the arm of the* VISITOR FROM THE ANTI-WORLD, *who disappears at once.*

JOSÉPHINE: Look! Is that who you meant? I saw him!

MARTHE: Yes, that's him.

BÉRENGER: Oh, so you saw him this time, did you?

JOSÉPHINE: But he was quite clear. I could even describe him. I can't think why that Englishwoman said what she saw was indescribable. This is a proof that goes against her. So her proof wasn't a proper one. What I saw had an arm, a pipe, a profile, a cap. . . .

MARTHE: No, not a cap. A tall hat.

BÉRENGER: Now be careful, this character is not like the one we saw. We can't possibly know what he's really like.

Enter JOHN BULL *from the left. He crosses the stage to go out on the right, smoking his fat cigar and without saying a word.*

Even if he's from the Anti-World the nearest to our own, he still can't have white hair, it must be black. The only picture we can see is like a negative. If he seems old to us, perhaps it's because he's really young, and then what do "actually" and "really" really mean? Let's stick to our own world. (*As he says the last two words, he looks at his daughter.*)

JOSÉPHINE: It's better that way.

BÉRENGER: You're still too young to understand all this. Anyway Sunday's not the time for philosophy.

MARTHE: Is this gentleman what people call a ghost?

The two OLD LADIES *come in from the right.*

BÉRENGER: It's a popular belief that when people die they go to the Anti-World.

FIRST LADY: There are a few little facts that seem to confirm this belief. As soon as someone passes on and is put into a coffin, the dead body disappears.

SECOND LADY: And that explains why coffins weigh so little. What happens to the bodies?

The Second English couple enter from the right.

SECOND MAN: What happens to the bodies? There's no such thing as ghosts.

A Stroll in the Air / 51

The First English couple appear from the left.

FIRST WOMAN: There's no such thing as ghosts.

BÉRENGER: Those who leave us settle down, so to speak, for good in the Anti-World, and they have anti-heads...

SECOND WOMAN: They have anti-heads.

Enter JOHN BULL *from the right.*

JOHN BULL: Anti-heads, anti-limbs, anti-clothes, anti-feelings and anti-hearts.

BÉRENGER: If we catch a glimpse of one, it's only by accident, like that pseudo-gentleman just now who was just a casual visitor.

FIRST WOMAN: So if there's no such thing as ghosts, we can still have casual visitors.

SECOND LADY: Or re-visitors.

FIRST LADY: So they just pass through one little corner of our universe by mistake, for a few seconds, almost without realizing.

FIRST WOMAN: Perhaps at this very moment *we* are paying *them* a visit.

SECOND WOMAN: Without knowing it.

JOHN BULL: But in that case how do we appear to them? Like nothing on earth.

JOSÉPHINE: These visitors are just fancies blown up by the winds.

THE ENGLISH CHARACTERS (*together, talking among themselves*): It seems these visitors are fancies blown up by the winds.

52 / *Eugène Ionesco*

FIRST WOMAN: Fancies blown up by the winds.

The English characters disperse and leave from both sides of the stage.

BÉRENGER: No, no, it's not true, the negative of our universe *does* exist, and we have proof of it, or rather it's our language that suggests the proof.

JOSÉPHINE: What proof does language suggest?

BÉRENGER: Well, for example, the expression "The world turned upside down" comes from there.... Although most people don't know its origin.

BÉRENGER, *with* JOSÉPHINE *and* MARTHE, *is now at the center of the stage.*

The objects that are now indicated by BÉRENGER *will appear either at the front of the stage, between* BÉRENGER *and the audience, or behind* BÉRENGER, *in front of the screen at the back, carried along on rails.*

BÉRENGER: ... Perhaps we can get a vague idea of this world when we see the turrets of a castle reflected in the water, or a fly upside down on the ceiling, or handwriting that you read from right to left or up the page, or an anagram (*this can be represented by a placard showing capital letters all jumbled up*), or a juggler or an acrobat, or the sun's rays shining through a crystal prism, reflected and broken up, disintegrating into a patchwork of colors and then put together again, you see, on this wall, on that screen, on your face, like a dazzling white light ... as though turned inside out ... it's a good thing the center of our universe doesn't collide with the center of the Anti-World....

MARTHE: What would happen then?

BÉRENGER: Then there'd be disintegration and annihilation for both. Pessimists even think that all the universes might destroy one another. The end of everything may come about like that.

MARTHE: Do you think so? That's terrible. And then what? There'd be nothing left?

BÉRENGER: We'd have to start again from the beginning.

JOSÉPHINE: Listen, *chéri,* I've been thinking! For quite a time now you've been drinking too much. It stops you working.

BÉRENGER: No, it doesn't. What do you think I'm doing now?

JOSÉPHINE: Well, the best you can say is that it inspires you to write purple patches like the one you've just been reciting.

MARTHE: Oh, leave him alone! He's free to do as he likes.

JOSÉPHINE: Come along! Instead of rambling on with all that nonsense, we'd better all go for a walk on the downs. The grass will freshen up your ideas.

BÉRENGER: Let's go for a stroll, yes, let's go for a stroll.

He takes JOSÉPHINE *and* MARTHE *by the hand; all three make for the back of the stage, where there is a bush or a tree in blossom.* JOSÉPHINE *is on Bérenger's left,* MARTHE *on his right.*

Suddenly, to the left of JOSÉPHINE *a small, pink, flower-covered column rises from the ground.*

JOSÉPHINE (*slightly alarmed*): What on earth is that?

BÉRENGER: You can see it's a column, can't you?

54 / *Eugène Ionesco*

MARTHE: It's wobbling about.

BÉRENGER: It's learning how to stand up straight.

JOSÉPHINE: It wasn't there a moment ago.

BÉRENGER: Of course not, it's just emerged from the void. You see, it's still quite fresh.

JOSÉPHINE: And what is the void?

BÉRENGER: It's a working hypothesis of the cosmos.

While he is talking, MARTHE *is picking daisies round about.*

You can't say it really exists, for if it existed, it wouldn't be void any longer. It's a kind of box. Every world and everything in these worlds goes into it and comes out of it, and yet it's very tiny, tinier than the tiniest cavity, tinier than the tiniest hollow in dice, tinier than tininess itself, because it has no dimension at all. You see, ruins like these, a relic of palaces that have ceased to exist, will be entirely swept away, of course, but perhaps, perhaps—and that's where there's a glimmer of hope—when they've passed through the void, they'll all be reconstructed and restored on the other side; inside out, naturally, as it's on the other side. Perhaps the rebuilding has already started; the stones and the ruins that disappear are being put together again out there. And the same with everything. And everything's aware of this, and that's what explains the happiness all about us, this feeling of victory (*he indicates both sides of the stage*), the beauty of the day.

The tree which had appeared at the back and which the BÉRENGER FAMILY *were making for, suddenly disappears.*

MARTHE: There's no tree any more. What's happened to the tree?

BÉRENGER: I expect it's been sucked back into the void.

JOSÉPHINE: That's really going a bit too far . . . !

BÉRENGER: No, it's quite natural.

JOSÉPHINE: How do you explain it then?

BÉRENGER: It's to restore the balance of things.

JOSÉPHINE: What balance?

BÉRENGER: Balance? I mean the balance that exists between the world and the outer worlds. If one thing leaves us (*The column disappears again.*) another must return. (*The tree reappears.*) For all these objects are the properties of the cosmos, they are all accounted for, there may be several infinities, but there are finite things within the infinite . . . the limits of infinity.

MARTHE: Why yes, *Maman*. I understand. Papa's explaining the accountancy of a multiple universe.

Fresh disappearance of the tree and fresh reappearance of the column.

BÉRENGER: The accountants are playing a game: one (*disappearance of the column*), two. (*Appearance of the tree.*) One, two. (*The trick is repeated.*)

MARTHE: Oh! Isn't that funny!

JOSÉPHINE: You think so, do you?

BÉRENGER: One. (*The tree and the column have disappeared at the same time.*) Well I never! Two. (*The tree and the column appear at the same time.*) An error in calculation, the accountant has made a mistake ... unless it's the property man.

Appearance of the figure of the VISITOR FROM THE ANTI-WORLD.

MARTHE: It's all because of him, it's his fault that everything's got mixed up.

JOSÉPHINE: There's no sense in it at all.

Disappearance of the VISITOR FROM THE ANTI-WORLD, *disappearance also of the tree and the column.*

There, you see, there are no rules, you can't make any rules for it.

BÉRENGER: Oh yes, you can.

JOSÉPHINE: Oh no, you can't, you can see for yourself.

Reappearance of the tree.

BÉRENGER: Oh yes, you can, you can see for yourself, what did I tell you?

MARTHE: What did Papa tell you?

Two or three successive disappearances and reappearances first of the tree, then of the column.

JOSÉPHINE: They get on my nerves, anyway. What do they think they're doing?

BÉRENGER: They're waiting for you to choose. Just make up your mind, that's all. Which do you prefer?

JOSÉPHINE: I'd rather have this one. (*She indicates the column, which now remains.*)

BÉRENGER: Well, keep the column then. I'll make you a present of it.

JOSÉPHINE: Thanks. But what do I have to do to make it stay?

MARTHE: It's when you want it, you make it stay!

BÉRENGER: The frontiers of the void are invisible, you can easily step the other side. Look!

The leg of the VISITOR FROM THE ANTI-WORLD *and his pipe appear and then disappear.*

Look!

Reappearance and fresh disappearance of the same character, this time headless and pipeless.

Look!

JOSÉPHINE: You're not going to bring him into it again! I told you I didn't want to see him any more.

BÉRENGER (*aside*): And to think there are people who imagine the void is like a huge black hole, a bottomless pit: and yet the void is neither black nor white and to be bottomless, it would need acres and acres and acres of space.

JOSÉPHINE: I told you I never wanted to see that gentleman again. Whether he's from our world or any other world, he gets on my nerves, he and his blessed pipe.

BÉRENGER (*still aside*): Yes. The void is neither white nor black, it doesn't exist, it's everywhere.

JOSÉPHINE: My dear man, are you with us? In the void or in the next world? I'm talking to you and you don't answer.

BÉRENGER: How do you manage to read my thoughts?

JOSÉPHINE: Because I'm an attentive wife. I was listening to you. I *do* listen to you, you know.

BÉRENGER: But I wasn't thinking out loud. I never even moved my lips.

JOSÉPHINE: That doesn't stop people from hearing if they really try.

MARTHE (*coming up to them with her bunch of daisies*): One's only got to look at you to guess everything you're thinking. You've got such an expressive face. You ought to be a film actor, or a mime or a monkey. Do you like my flowers?

BÉRENGER: They're so full of life you can hear them breathe.

MARTHE: Would you like one? (*She puts a flower in his buttonhole.*) It's the most beautiful one. (*Turning to* JOSÉPHINE:) Would you like one, or two? (MARTHE *puts the flowers on Joséphine's hat.*)

BÉRENGER: I never could resist a loving gesture. Ah! If only everyone was like you! Then we'd all be so gentle. Life would be possible and we'd even die peacefully, without regrets. If you live happily, you can die happily. We always ought to love one another.

JOSÉPHINE: It does happen occasionally, after all.

MARTHE: I'm always full of love.

BÉRENGER: What do you love?

MARTHE: I love . . . I don't know what I love. . . . But I'm full of love. Everything you can see around you is so beautiful.

BÉRENGER: You're right. But we forget. Most of the time we forget. Remind me again, when you see us looking worried, your mother and me.

JOSÉPHINE (*to* MARTHE): Mind you don't drop your flowers. (*To* BÉRENGER:) Where are we going to put this column? On the balcony or in the courtyard?

BÉRENGER: I've never been so relaxed; I've never been so happy. I've never felt so light, so weightless. What's happening to me?

While he is speaking to MARTHE, *the scenery changes; the column quietly disappears.*

It's all because of you. You were right, you know.

JOSÉPHINE: I think it's the air that does you good. The oxygen. You ought to live more often in the country. The doctor's told you before. And then it's the walking too, everyone knows that.

BÉRENGER: I suppose it's that, I suppose it must be that. When I look around me, it's as though I was seeing everything for the first time. As though I'd just been born.

JOSÉPHINE: Well, now you know. In the future you've only got to keep your eyes open.

BÉRENGER: It's... how can I explain it? Like some feeling of joy that's been forgotten, forgotten yet still familiar, like something that's belonged to me from the beginning of time. You lose it every day and yet it's never really lost. And the proof is that you can find it again, that you can recognize it. That's what it is.

JOSÉPHINE: Don't get so excited. There's no need to go hopping about like a child.

60 / *Eugène Ionesco*

MARTHE: Oh, it doesn't matter. No one can see him. There are no English people about.

JOSÉPHINE (*to* BÉRENGER): It's all a bit abstract, what you're saying.

BÉRENGER: No, on the contrary, it's all very concrete. This happiness is something physical. I can feel it *here*. The air that fills my lungs is more rarefied than air. It gives off vapors that are going to my head. A sort of divine intoxication! Divinely intoxicated! Can you feel it too? Do you feel it too?

JOSÉPHINE: A little, perhaps.

MARTHE: I do, quite a lot.

JOSÉPHINE: Isn't it rather disturbing? I'm afraid *I* find it rather disturbing.

BÉRENGER: At the moment, no. I have no more worries. No worries at all.

JOSÉPHINE: Well then, *you're* all right! So long as it lasts!

BÉRENGER: My head is reeling with conviction.

JOSÉPHINE: What conviction?

MARTHE: Don't ask him any more questions, *Maman*, it might shake his convictions.

BÉRENGER: Conviction, conviction. I don't know what conviction, but I'm convinced it *is* a conviction.

JOSÉPHINE: Well, it can't be a conviction. If it's so vague and imprecise, it's a very unconvincing conviction. It's in the nature of a conviction to be precise.

BÉRENGER: For me, for me, once a conviction's been

limited by definition, it isn't one any more. Give it frontiers and it's invaded by doubt and denial. Anyway, there's nothing more imprecise than precision.

JOSÉPHINE: You ought to read Descartes again.

BÉRENGER: What is the precise meaning of precision?

JOSÉPHINE: You speak a very peculiar language of your own. With you words no longer mean anything. They're quite unrecognizable.

MARTHE: Not to me.

JOSÉPHINE: Oh, be quiet! You don't have to agree with everything he says, without thinking, just because he's your father. (*To* BÉRENGER:) No one can understand you but yourself. And I sometimes wonder!

MARTHE: *I* understand him.

JOSÉPHINE: That's just your luck!

BÉRENGER: Even if I don't understand myself what's it matter? I wouldn't be so happy if I understood.

JOSÉPHINE: Anyway, there must be some reason for it.

BÉRENGER: Yes, there may be a reason, after all. Let's go on with our walk.

JOSÉPHINE: Let's walk, then, that won't do us any harm.

MARTHE: Let's walk. Give me your hand, Papa, and yours, Maman.

They turn around, take each other by the hand and take a few steps toward the back of the stage. A very large silver bridge appears on the screen, which has gone on moving occasionally during the conversation, showing various different landscapes.

BÉRENGER: That's it, that's the reason for it, it's all because of that. Look! Look at it! (BÉRENGER *runs a few steps away from the others toward the bridge.*)

JOSÉPHINE: Where are you going?

MARTHE: Wait for us. Where are you running to? Don't go away!

JOSÉPHINE: Wait for us!

Then, seeing the silver bridge, JOSÉPHINE *and* MARTHE *both cry out.*

JOSÉPHINE AND MARTHE: Oh! How beautiful!

JOSÉPHINE: It's magnificent!

MARTHE: You see, he *was* right.

JOSÉPHINE: That's true, Bérenger, you weren't wrong after all.

The silver bridge, dazzlingly brilliant, joins the two sides of the gorge above the abyss. It is like some ship in the shape of an arch, which seems to be suspended very high in the air above the river, leaping from one gleaming hilltop to the other.

MARTHE *and* JOSÉPHINE *have also gone closer to the back of the stage and gaze at it.*

The English characters, with their children, have come in from left and right. They also gaze at the bridge. But they are more phlegmatic, much more phlegmatic, and their reactions are more reasonable.

BÉRENGER: I understand, now I understand why I feel so happy. That's why I felt so light and airy just now.

A Stroll in the Air / 63

FIRST MAN (*entering from the left*): Oh!

FIRST WOMAN: Ah!

SECOND MAN (*entering from the opposite side to the* FIRST MAN): Ah!

SECOND WOMAN: Oh!

JOHN BULL (*entering from the left*): Ahoh!

LITTLE BOY (*who is coming with his parents*): What is that great big thing?

FIRST LADY: You mustn't call it a great big thing. You see, we call it a great silver bridge.

JOURNALIST (*coming in from the left*): Ah! There you are, Monsieur Bérenger, could you say a few words about this bridge?

JOSÉPHINE: Leave him alone, Monsieur, he's not an engineer, he's not an architect, he knows nothing about structures.

JOURNALIST: I beg your pardon, Madame, I apologize.

(*He withdraws.*)

MARTHE: Now we can't see anything. All these English people have gone and stood in the way.

JOSÉPHINE: Mesdames, Messieurs, do you mind moving aside? *We* saw it first.

All the English people, one after the other, say "I'm sorry" and move aside. The LITTLE GIRL *says "I'm sorry" too, but not the* LITTLE BOY.

FIRST WOMAN: Will you say "I'm sorry" or I'll slap your behind!

LITTLE BOY: I don't want to say I'm sorry.

FIRST WOMAN (*to* JOSÉPHINE): I *am* sorry.

The silver bridge, which was hidden for a time by the English people, reappears still more brilliant and beautiful. On the hillside opposite, on either side of the bridge, you can see the stations of the rack railway and the telpher cabins moving backward and forward all in different colors. The silver arch should catch and reflect the sun's rays and the brilliance of the sky, dazzlingly intensified.

JOSÉPHINE: Why do they seem so surprised? It's *their* bridge, it's in their own country, they can look at it every day.

FIRST MAN: We only look at it on our days off, that's quite enough.

SECOND MAN: In France, no one would look at it at all.

Little motorcars start crossing the bridge at full speed. The light is reflected in the car windows and flashes back, broken into a thousand rainbow-colored fragments.

MARTHE: What are those moving lights? You'd think they were diamonds flashing along.

BÉRENGER: I expect they're those famous particles of light that scientists call "photons."

JOURNALIST: Although they say the French love to stand and stare.

MARTHE: Is that true?

FIRST WOMAN: There are some enormous bridges in America too, but the Americans cross them with their eyes shut.

JOSÉPHINE: You'll make her more stupid than she is already. She takes you seriously, you know.

SECOND LADY: That's why there are so many accidents, that's why they crash over the top.

MARTHE: I know he's only joking.

FIRST LADY: There are some in Russia too.

JOHN BULL: I've seen two in Australia as well.

JOSÉPHINE: When does he ever stop joking? Still, I suppose it's better when he is. It's only when he's miserable that he stops talking nonsense.

FIRST LADY: But no one looks at them there. No one takes much interest, it appears.

JOHN BULL: People are only interested in their practical utility.

MARTHE: Are you often miserable? Oh! it makes me feel miserable to know you're miserable.

FIRST WOMAN: And that means the bridge no longer exists.

SECOND MAN: It's destructive to be too practical.

BÉRENGER (*gaily, jumping up and down*): I feel miserable when I think of the years going by like a lot of sacks we send back empty. I feel miserable when I think we're all going to leave one another and even take leave of ourselves. But hollow hours are made for sorrow. And today I'm filled with joy, overflowing with happiness. (BÉRENGER *goes on jumping up and down while he says this and makes sweeping gestures with his arms, like wings.*)

SECOND WOMAN: Destructive of what?

SECOND MAN: Destructive of everything.

JOHN BULL: It's an admirable piece of English construction.

JOURNALIST: It dates from the time of Mary Stuart.

JOSÉPHINE (*using her lorgnette to cover her embarrassment*): Mind what you're doing! They're looking at you.

The English characters have indeed turned around to face the public and they gaze at BÉRENGER, *vaguely disapproving.*

Don't get so excited! You get too carried away. Your excitability's much too Latin for their latitude. It's not nice. It's ridiculous.

JOURNALIST: But it had to be restored.

FIRST LADY: They don't make any like it nowadays.

BÉRENGER (*hopping and jumping up and down*): Forgive me, Joséphine. I can't help it. Forgive me, ladies and gentlemen, I feel so gay I can't control it. I'm overflowing.

JOHN BULL: He feels so gay he can't control it.

FIRST MAN: He's overflowing.

BÉRENGER: I'm transported, carried away.

THE ENGLISHMEN: Transported!

THE ENGLISHWOMEN: Carried away!

FIRST WOMAN (*to the* LITTLE BOY): This gentleman's French, you see.

A Stroll in the Air / 67

LITTLE GIRL: Why is that gentleman hopping up and down?

BÉRENGER: I'm overflowing, transported, carried away, lifted right off the ground. (*Bérenger's feet have indeed lifted a few inches from the ground.*)

JOSÉPHINE: Don't talk so loud, Bérenger.

BÉRENGER: The soles of my shoes are just brushing the top of the grass!

JOSÉPHINE: But what on earth do you think you're doing? Stop it!

BÉRENGER (*to the English characters*): Have you noticed anything?

FIRST MAN: He looks happy enough.

FIRST WOMAN: What's he doing?

JOURNALIST: He's walking very fast.

SECOND WOMAN: It looks as if he's gliding. Yes, he *is* gliding.

SECOND MAN: I think he's pretending to ski or to skate.

FIRST LADY: He's enjoying himself because it's Sunday.

SECOND LADY: We ought to enjoy ourselves on Sundays. But there's no need to caper about like a mad thing.

JOSÉPHINE: They say you must be mad.

LITTLE BOY: You'd almost think he'd grown. Grownups can grow too. (*To his mother:*) Do you still go on growing when you're grown up?

JOHN BULL: Perhaps. Perhaps he *has* grown an inch or two at the most. In England, there's nothing very strange about that. (*To* JOSÉPHINE:) Don't let it worry you, Madame.

JOSÉPHINE: It's impossible. It's crazy.

JOURNALIST: It's hardly noticeable to us. We're usually very tall. Much taller than that.

SECOND MAN: He'll never be as tall as us.

FIRST MAN: Or, at any rate, not for long.

BÉRENGER *has his feet on the ground again.*

You see, he's just an average height again now.

BÉRENGER *is again lifted from the ground.*

MARTHE: Isn't it funny! Papa's walking above the grass. He's really walking over the top of the grass.

JOSÉPHINE: Oh, be quiet! You're mad. They'll start making fun of us.

The two children start hopping about.

FIRST WOMAN (*to her son*): Now, be a good boy! What do you think you're doing?

SECOND MAN (*to his daughter*): You mustn't hop about like this, that's no way to behave.

FIRST MAN: It's the terrible education they get at school. It's not like it used to be.

JOSÉPHINE: Now look here, Bérenger, you're setting a very bad example.

MARTHE: But he is, yes he is, he's walking over the top of the grass.

JOSÉPHINE *gazes at Bérenger's feet with her lorgnette.*

A Stroll in the Air / 69

Look at the grass, and look at his feet!

JOSÉPHINE: But you're quite right. It's perfectly true. (*To* BÉRENGER:) It's not respectable, do you hear? What on earth do you think you're doing? Herbert, have you finished?

FIRST LADY: It's his way of showing he's happy. (*To* JOSÉPHINE:) Leave him alone, Madame, and let him enjoy himself.

JOHN BULL: There are a thousand ways of showing you're happy. But there's no need to show it at all.

SECOND MAN: We'd rather be reserved.

JOURNALIST: It's one aspect of his personality. I'll make a note of that.

FIRST WOMAN: He's an artist.

FIRST LADY: I find it rather charming and original.

JOHN BULL: That is not my opinion.

FIRST MAN: After all, he *is* a guest.

JOSÉPHINE: Herbert! Herbert!

FIRST MAN: As he's a guest, let's say no more about it.

JOSÉPHINE: He's almost a foot above the ground! We'll be a laughing stock! You'll make us all look ridiculous.

JOHN BULL: I can't help thinking he's rather ill-bred.

The two OLD ENGLISH LADIES *start hopping about like our feathered friends.*

FIRST MAN: It's odd for someone from the Continent. He ought to have his feet on the ground.

70 / *Eugène Ionesco*

SECOND MAN: Perhaps it's that disease they call St. Vitus's dance.

FIRST MAN (*to the* JOURNALIST): What do you make of it?

JOURNALIST: Modern man is quite unbalanced. As you can see in behavior like this.

JOHN BULL (*looking at the* OLD LADIES): And as for them, they look like a lot of old hens. You see, it's infectious too.

FIRST WOMAN: I can't think how people can let themselves go like that and make an exhibition of themselves. (*She starts hopping about like a bird too, and says to the* LITTLE BOY *who is now quite still:*) That's enough! I tell you that's enough!

SECOND WOMAN: Neither can I. (*She also begins to hop about.*)

FIRST MAN: Our wives are light in the head.

SECOND MAN: They're unforgivably light on their feet.

The two Englishmen also start hopping about.

SECOND WOMAN (*hopping about, to the* LITTLE GIRL, *who is now quite still*): That's enough now! That's enough!

JOURNALIST: We ought to put these foreigners from the Continent in quarantine or at least vaccinate them before we let them in. (*He too begins to hop about.*)

JOHN BULL: That's what happens when you let your body get out of hand. It's very infectious. (*He lumbers about with the others.*)

BÉRENGER *and his family are now the only ones who are not hopping about; the children and the others still go on with it for a few moments.*

JOSÉPHINE (*to* BÉRENGER): Everyone says the same thing. They'll all think you've been badly brought up. (*To* MARTHE:) Whatever you do, don't you start.

MARTHE: Everyone's trying to do the same. But they can't. Papa's the most graceful.

JOSÉPHINE: They're only doing it out of politeness. (*To* BÉRENGER:) You look so badly brought up.

JOHN BULL (*with a thick, rather singsong voice*): No, no, you look so badly brought up.

BÉRENGER: I'll bring myself up a bit higher in a minute.

JOSÉPHINE: They'll attack you in the newspapers. You'll never get another English visa.

The other English characters sing in chorus: "No, no, you've been so badly brought up." All movement ceases.

BÉRENGER: I feel uplifted and submerged by joy.

JOSÉPHINE (*to* MARTHE): What did he say?

MARTHE: Didn't you hear? He's been flooded. Uplifted and submerged by joy.

All the following passage is sung.

JOHN BULL: What did he say?

TWO LADIES: What did he say?

THE TWO ENGLISHMEN AND THE JOURNALIST: What did he say?

LITTLE GIRL (*solo*): He's been uplifted and submerged by joy. There's nothing wrong with that.

BÉRENGER *leaps about, looking as though he was gliding through the water. End of the sung section.*

FIRST LADY: He's walking way above the ground. . . .

SECOND LADY: And you'd almost think he was gliding through the water, prancing along on his seahorse, on a gigantic hippocampus.

FIRST WOMAN: Along the bottom of the ocean.

JOURNALIST: The air this morning is almost as heavy as water.

SECOND MAN: And the blue sky . . .

JOHN BULL (*singing*): And our English sky is a deep-sea Navy blue.

JOSÉPHINE: You might at least explain it to us.

JOURNALIST: That strange habit of his, those eccentric movements demand an explanation.

SECOND MAN (*to* BÉRENGER): Excuse me, Monsieur, but I can't help thinking you ought to explain yourself.

FIRST WOMAN: He's going to explain.

THE ENGLISH CHARACTERS (*in spoken chorus*): The foreign visitor wants to explain himself.

JOSÉPHINE: Well go on, Herbert, explain yourself!

THE TWO OLD LADIES: Explain yourself, Monsieur, and be a welcome guest.

THE ENGLISHMEN: Explain yourself, Mr. Foreigner!

THE ENGLISHWOMEN: Explain yourself!

JOURNALIST: Are you bringing us a new epidemic?

> BÉRENGER *seems to be having great difficulty in keeping to the surface of the ground. From time to time he makes a few easy little leaps.*

BÉRENGER: No, you can see for yourself, I'm flying.

JOURNALIST: He says he's flying.

BÉRENGER: I've found the way to do it again, the way we'd all forgotten. (*He leaps three feet into the air.*)

FIRST MAN: He says he's found the way to do it again.

FIRST WOMAN: What has he found the way to do?

JOURNALIST: He says he's found the way to fly again.

BÉRENGER *makes a leap of six feet into the air.*

JOSÉPHINE: Now you've gone far enough. You're not a butterfly.

JOHN BULL: It's not natural.

MARTHE: He's not a caterpillar either.

FIRST MAN: No, it's not natural.

BÉRENGER: I promise you, it's all quite spontaneous. It just happens all by itself.

FIRST LADY: If it just happens, perhaps it's natural after all.

JOSÉPHINE: You're out of your mind.

BÉRENGER (*standing still*): Man has a crying need to fly.

JOHN BULL: I don't believe you.

BÉRENGER: It's as necessary and as natural as breathing.

FIRST MAN: You mean we've a crying need to *eat*.

SECOND MAN: And then to drink.

JOURNALIST: And then to philosophize.

FIRST WOMAN: And then if there's any time left . . .

SECOND WOMAN: Then perhaps we'll fly, just for fun.

JOSÉPHINE: Everyone thinks you're wrong.

BÉRENGER: But I'm not, I'm not, everyone knows how to fly. It's an innate gift, but everyone forgets. How could I have forgotten the way it's done? It's so simple, so clear, so childish. It would be better for us to starve than not to fly. I expect that's why we all feel so unhappy.

FIRST MAN: I don't feel in the least unhappy.

FIRST WOMAN: It's true we'd save lots of money if we knew how to fly.

JOHN BULL: It would be the end of industry.

BÉRENGER: You *are* unhappy, but you don't know it. That's what's wrong with mankind: we've forgotten how to fly. What would you say if we'd forgotten how to swim or walk or sit or stand?

JOHN BULL: Sitting's good enough for me. But I like standing too. Or lying flat on my tum with my backside as a blanket.

SECOND LADY: Supposing we did know how to do it once, Monsieur, we'd never be able to learn how to fly again now, it's too late.

JOSÉPHINE: It's too late.

BÉRENGER: It's never too late. Besides, all you have to do is remember.

JOURNALIST: Nowadays, science won't let us rely entirely on our memory. It's even better not to rely on it at all. It's not reliable. It's misleading.

FIRST MAN: If there really are people who fly, they must all be mad.

JOURNALIST: And worse!

SECOND MAN: Not all of them, anyway.

JOURNALIST: People who've gone right around the bend.

JOHN BULL: The incurable, the hopeless cases.

JOSÉPHINE: I've never seen him do this before. Believe me, he can still surprise me, even after all these years of married life.

BÉRENGER: If most of the time I've forgotten how to fly, I still feel I ought to be able to. I know what it is that's missing and makes me suffer. It's like not keeping fit. If we don't fly, it's because we're not healthy enough.

FIRST LADY: I must say, ladies and gentlemen, it would seem that if we invent rockets and airplanes and interspatial machines, it must be because men feel they *ought* to fly.

SECOND LADY: We're trying to fulfill a crying need.

JOURNALIST: Technology has adequately and brilliantly fulfilled that need already.

JOSÉPHINE: You can't do better than technology.

BÉRENGER: Does a cripple in a wheel chair really walk?

MARTHE: No, he's pushed along.

BÉRENGER: Does a motorist walk?

JOURNALIST: He rolls along on wheels, Monsieur.

BÉRENGER: He rolls along, shut up in a little box. It's the box that rolls *him* along.

FIRST MAN: But a pilot, a pilot, you mean to say a pilot doesn't fly?

FIRST WOMAN: That's right, that's what my husband says. You can't say a pilot doesn't fly?

BÉRENGER: He doesn't fly.

LITTLE BOY: Yes, Monsieur, he does.

FIRST MAN: Shut up!

FIRST WOMAN: It's not polite to interrupt grownups when they're talking.

BÉRENGER: No, he doesn't fly. It's his machine that flies.

JOSÉPHINE: You'll never be able to compete with aviation.

JOHN BULL: He'd like us to break up all our planes and sink all our ships.

SECOND WOMAN (*to the* JOURNALIST): Perhaps he's a spy in England, an enemy agent.

FIRST MAN: Where will it all lead us, anyway?

SECOND MAN: To the calamity of calamities.

BÉRENGER: It's as easy to fly as to breathe.

JOURNALIST: No, it's certainly not as easy to fly as to breathe.

BÉRENGER: Oh yes, it is!

MARTHE: I think it's just as easy to fly as to breathe.

JOSÉPHINE: Don't be silly, of course it isn't!

JOHN BULL: Even if it was, we oughtn't to.

SECOND LADY: Why not, as it's natural?

FIRST LADY: I'm not at all sure it *is* natural, my dear.

SECOND LADY: And everything that's natural is nice.

A Stroll in the Air / 77

JOHN BULL: We should rise above our instincts.

BÉRENGER: We rise above them when we fly over them. We ought to have our own means of flying, our own means.

FIRST MAN: No, we shouldn't.

FIRST LADY: Perhaps we should.

SECOND MAN: No, madam.

LITTLE GIRL: Yes.

SECOND MAN: No.

FIRST LADY: Yes.

JOHN BULL: No.

THE TWO OLD LADIES (*together*): Yes, yes.

THE ENGLISHMEN: No.

THE TWO OLD LADIES: Of course we should.

THE ENGLISHWOMEN: Perhaps we should.

JOURNALIST: But what if we really could? We've only just seen, it would only help us to jump across roads and gardens and rivers . . .

FIRST MAN: . . . and bushes and one-story houses. . . .

SECOND MAN: Like a wretched little cricket.

JOHN BULL: Man is not a cricket.

BÉRENGER: Man can fly much higher than a cricket. In the old days he used to. We've just got to catch the habit again, I tell you, get back into the habit.

MARTHE: Perhaps we only lost it because we're lazy.

78 / Eugène Ionesco

BÉRENGER: I don't call it progress to walk on crutches. If we're not careful we'll forget how to walk too. It's started already, anyway. We're losing all our natural powers.

JOURNALIST: On the contrary, technology multiplies them.

BÉRENGER: There's nothing on the roads now but cars.

FIRST LADY: It's true, there are very few pedestrians left.

SECOND LADY: And no one thinks much of *them*!

FIRST LADY: Soon, they'll have all disappeared.

SECOND LADY: We'll have all disappeared.

BÉRENGER: I want to remain a pedestrian and a pedestrian in the air. (*He takes a leap.*) I want to stroll in the air without any artificial mechanical aid. (*He takes another leap.*)

FIRST WOMAN: Good Heavens! He's off again!

MARTHE: How do you do it? Teach me!

JOURNALIST: He'll never go any higher.

FIRST MAN: He's shown us all he's able to do.

SECOND MAN: And that's not much.

JOHN BULL: All right, if he thinks he can go any higher, he can prove it to us.

JOSÉPHINE: Everyone says you can't go any higher. So don't try. It's not worth it. Relax.

BÉRENGER: Oh yes, I can. So can you all, we can all do it. I'll tell you what you must do.

FIRST LADY: He's going to tell us what we must do.

A Stroll in the Air / 79

SECOND LADY: What did he say?

FIRST LADY: He said he's going to tell us what we must do.

JOHN BULL: In so far as politeness permits, permit me to permit us all to laugh.

BÉRENGER: It's perfectly simple. All you need is the will to do it. You've got to have confidence. You only come down when you lose confidence. You may have noticed that when you come down you never drop like a stone.

SECOND LADY: That's true. I remember that.

JOURNALIST: You mean you *seem* to remember it.

BÉRENGER: It's just another proof that it's perfectly natural to fly. And when you're in full flight, away above the highest trees or over a lake or a hilltop, you never feel frightened. Whereas, in an airplane, you often *do*.

FIRST WOMAN: And even in a cable railway.

FIRST LADY: I'm even afraid on my balcony, I get so dizzy.

BÉRENGER: But of course sometimes you feel terribly surprised to be flying right over the cathedral, the roofs and the mountains.

SECOND MAN: What happens if you start feeling too surprised?

BÉRENGER: Once you start thinking it's not normal to stay up there in the air without wings and a propeller, then your faith is shaken, you lose height and you come down, but no faster than a lift. Sometimes you can shoot up and climb again by an effort of will, as though you were throwing out ballast. But not for long. It only needs a little crack in your will power and you start gliding right down to earth. Whenever I've found the secret again in myself, how many times have I said as I threw myself into the air: "Now I know and I'll always know, I'll never forget, any more than I can forget how to look or to listen."

A child's red balloon can be seen coming gently down from the flies to the stage.

This time I really won't forget. I'll be careful, I'll remember, I'll jot down all my movements in a notebook, then I can reproduce them whenever I like. (*He leaps very easily into the air.*) I can't stay down any longer. I'm longing to take the air and go higher and higher up. I'm going to fly right over this valley. I want to see what there is in the other valleys, the other side of those hills.

FIRST LADY: He can hardly hold himself down.

FIRST WOMAN: He's like a restless horse pawing the ground.

SECOND WOMAN: Look at him! He's only touching the ground with the tips of his toes.

FIRST WOMAN: He's going up.

BÉRENGER *rises nearly a couple of feet and comes down again.*

FIRST MAN: He's coming down again.

SECOND LADY: He's going up again.

SECOND MAN: He's coming down again.

JOSÉPHINE (*to* MARTHE): Tell him to stop. He won't listen to *me*. (*To* BÉRENGER:) Herbert, let's go home or we'll miss the train.

A Stroll in the Air / 81

MARTHE (*to her father*): How do you do it?

BÉRENGER: It's very easy, I'll show you.

JOSÉPHINE: That would be the last straw.

BÉRENGER: You'll see. It's a game. A children's game. Of course there are a few rules to obey, but they're simple ones. There are all sorts of little tricks. Let's see now, which shall I choose? You can swim in the air. But that's tiring. You can float on the air: but you don't go very high. If you know how to ride a bicycle, you can cycle up too. It's another machine, I know, but we've got so used to this one, it's the best way for beginners to learn. Machines are taking over the functions of men. Let's use one of these substitutes to rediscover one of man's lost functions.

A white circus bicycle is thrown on from the wings. BÉRENGER *catches it.*

At the same moment tiers of seats appear, like a circus, and the English characters and JOSÉPHINE *go and take their places there. They have become the audience at a circus.*

MARTHE *is on the right, at the front of the stage, with her back to the seats.*

It is not necessary for the circus to be constructed. It can be suggested by a few items. A platform, sloping upwards to the wings, could slide on from the left and acrobat rings can appear over the heads of the spectators, unless nylon wires are used to raise the acrobat.

While BÉRENGER *explains what must be done, he does it. He gets on the bicycle.*

82 / *Eugène Ionesco*

BÉRENGER: Look: you move your legs as though you're going to set the wheels in motion. You sit very straight, as though you've got a saddle. With your hands in front of you, as though they were on the handle bars. After seven or eight turns of the pedals, you gradually move off. (BÉRENGER *goes around the arena.*)

JOSÉPHINE: Move a bit further away, no one can see properly.

JOHN BULL: It's very easy.

JOURNALIST: Let's wait for what comes next.

BÉRENGER: And suddenly you find you're as high as a wardrobe . . . a young cherry tree . . . an older cherry tree.

LITTLE BOY: Is that gentleman a balloon?

THE ENGLISHWOMEN: Oh!

> BÉRENGER *will cycle around the stage right above the heads of the spectators, who will have to look up to see him. He could ride up the sloping platform, disappear in the wings, and then reappear still above the characters, possibly replaced by a trained acrobat.*
>
> *Acrobatic turn: the bicycle has only one wheel, then there are no handle bars.* BÉRENGER *goes on moving around in circles, still pedaling like a cyclist. Then he comes down again. And when he does the platform and the rings disappear.*

BÉRENGER: . . . and then a much older cherry tree. Like this, there you are. Understand? Try it.

> *While* BÉRENGER *is circling around on high in a clockwise direction,* MARTHE *is circling around below on another bicycle in an anti-clockwise direction.*

A Stroll in the Air / 83

JOSÉPHINE: Look out! Be careful! Don't listen to him!

When the two bicycles have disappeared and the circus turn is over, the English characters applaud; BÉRENGER *acknowledges the applause by raising his hands above his head like a champion.*

LITTLE BOY: Encore!

BÉRENGER (*to* MARTHE): You see, flying's as easy as riding a bike.

FIRST MAN: You've got to know how to ride one first. And *I* don't.

FIRST LADY: I know how.

LITTLE GIRL: You can learn at any age.

BÉRENGER (*to all*): You simply have to keep your balance.

JOHN BULL: I don't know how to ride a bike either.

FIRST WOMAN: You know how to ride a horse.

SECOND MAN: Not all horses have wings.

SECOND LADY: But a lot of them have. My husband had two in his stables with wings.

JOSÉPHINE: And he really used to go flying with them?

SECOND LADY: No, they were only ornamental.

JOHN BULL: I've never seen a horse with wings! And I've owned plenty of horses.

SECOND MAN: But it seems they really exist.

JOURNALIST: It's a special breed, but they're dying out.

The circus props have disappeared. The English have been getting up while they spoke.

Once again it is the countryside; bathed in a dazzling light. The silver arch can still be seen. No more scenes in the background. Just a kind of sky or blue void.

The English surround BÉRENGER, *but all keeping a fair distance between one another and* BÉRENGER *himself.*

JOHN BULL: In fact, he uses mechanical aids like anyone else.

FIRST MAN: A bicycle! That's not very smart!

SECOND MAN: Lots of people can ride a bike. And what's more, I don't envy them.

FIRST WOMAN: It's a pseudo-bicycle.

JOHN BULL: And that's even more uninteresting.

FIRST MAN: Even a flying bicycle is still a nasty creeping thing on wheels.

JOURNALIST: An unreal bicycle's no better than a real one.

BÉRENGER: There is a more natural method.

FIRST LADY: He says there's a more natural way.

BÉRENGER: A gymnastic method. (*To* MARTHE:) Watch closely.

Trapezes descend from the flies, in nylon if possible, unless BÉRENGER *is to be raised with nylon wires. As before,* BÉRENGER *will act out his explanations.*

MARTHE: Yes, Papa.

BÉRENGER: Here we go! You leap in the air as high as you can, lifting your arms right up. And then instead of jumping down again, you hang on to an imaginary

A Stroll in the Air / 85

branch, as though you were going to climb a tree. (*He jumps and remains about three feet above the ground.*) Then you pull yourself up by the strength of your wrists and catch on to another branch a little higher. (*He does this.*) And so you climb from branch to imaginary branch. (*He rises up in successive jerks.*) You can climb as high as you like. For the imaginary tree is as high as you want it to be. It's even infinitely high, if you like. If you can do it, you never *stop* climbing! Try it.

MARTHE *tries it.*

MARTHE: It's so difficult. I can't.

JOSÉPHINE: It's much too hard for her. She hasn't had any training. She's never been good at gym.

The LITTLE BOY *tries, but he can't do it either.*

BÉRENGER: Like this. (*He jerks himself up a little higher, then slowly comes down again.*) Of course it's hard to start with, and it's tiring, but the higher you climb, the easier it is. Some force pushes you up; you don't feel your own weight any more. You can scramble up with one hand. Or one finger. And then just thinking does it. (*One more easy leap; then* BÉRENGER *comes down again.*) Where there's a will there's a way. Where there's a will there's a way.

JOHN BULL: It's easy.

SECOND LADY: Do it then, if you can.

JOHN BULL: You've only got to be lighter than air. That's the only rule. But it's beneath my dignity.

JOURNALIST: What's more, it's risky, it's dangerous. The

natural resistance of the air tries to stop you rising. And you shouldn't fight against it.

FIRST MAN: You shouldn't weaken the forces that bring you down or you might get lightheaded. You can get just as drunk at high altitudes as you can in the lower depths.

SECOND WOMAN: You might disappear for good.

FIRST MAN: We mustn't destroy any of the forces of nature.

BÉRENGER: We mustn't resist them either, we mustn't resist them either. (*To everybody:*) You want to have a go? You want to try it? Do you want to fly with me?

The English characters move away protesting, except for the English children whose parents are tugging them away by the hand.

Don't be afraid! (*To* JOSÉPHINE *and to* MARTHE:) I can take each of you under one arm if you don't want to fly by yourselves.

JOSÉPHINE: But you're not going to take us by force.

FIRST MAN: You're not going to take this lady by force.

MARTHE: Well, *I* don't know. . . . I'd rather like to.

JOSÉPHINE: I absolutely forbid it.

JOURNALIST: We object.

JOHN BULL: With all our weight.

THE ENGLISH (*in chorus*): We object with all our weight.

Suddenly BÉRENGER, *hitting the ground a little too hard with his feet, takes flight and rapidly disappears in a flash into the flies.*

A Stroll in the Air / 87

JOSÉPHINE: He didn't do it on purpose. This time I'm sure he didn't do it on purpose.

MARTHE: Yes, he *did* do it on purpose.

THE ENGLISH (*together, gaze at him in the air*): Oh! Ah! Oh!

The LITTLE GIRL *starts singing a kind of English hymn.*

FIRST LADY: He hit the ground with his foot harder than he intended.

FIRST WOMAN: Look, he's going up very quickly!

SECOND MAN: I expect he's been sucked up by some rising current in the atmosphere.

JOSÉPHINE: He's mad. He's mad.

MARTHE (*to* JOSÉPHINE): Don't get so excited!

SECOND LADY: He's been swept up in a whirlwind.

FIRST MAN: He's slowing down.

SECOND MAN: He's going off at a tangent.

FIRST WOMAN: He's reached the calm waters of the air.

SECOND WOMAN: He's flying parallel with the arch.

LITTLE BOY: He's a balloon. He's a balloon.

FIRST LADY: But high above it.

SECOND LADY: Very much higher.

JOURNALIST: He doesn't need to make complicated movements now.

FIRST MAN: He's not making any movements at all.

88 / *Eugène Ionesco*

FIRST WOMAN: He's holding himself quite straight, he's motionless in the air.

JOHN BULL: What's he doing? What's he doing?

JOSÉPHINE: What *can* he be doing?

FIRST LADY: He's slowly making for that hill over there.

FIRST MAN: How does he manage to keep on the right course?

SECOND LADY: He just looks ahead. It's the way he looks that takes him in the right direction.

MARTHE: That's very good, Papa, bravo!

JOURNALIST: He's going higher still.

FIRST MAN: He's floating on his back.

SECOND MAN: He's flying very fast in a horizontal position.

FIRST WOMAN: He's veering to the right.

SECOND WOMAN: He's disappeared to the right.

FIRST LADY: Now he's coming back on the left.

SECOND LADY: There he is, straight ahead.

The English characters move their heads and turn completely around, very fast and comically, in order to follow him in his course.

JOURNALIST: He's disappeared again.

FIRST MAN: Now he's over there.

SECOND LADY: There he is again.

JOURNALIST (*to* JOSÉPHINE): And what do you make of your husband's exploits, Madame?

JOSÉPHINE: It upsets me. But I've every confidence.

ENGLISHMEN AND WOMEN: He's disappeared. He's reappeared. He's disappeared. He's circling around again.

In the background can be seen a sort of glowing ball or fireworks rocket, which appears and disappears, going from right to left and from left to right, faster and faster.

JOHN BULL: That's 36 times he's been around. 36 times.

SECOND WOMAN: 45.

FIRST LADY: 97.

FIRST MAN: No, 95.

FIRST LADY: 97.

SECOND WOMAN: We've all lost count. He's made a complete circuit more than 200 times.

MARTHE: He's going so fast you'd think he'd stopped moving.

The ball stops a moment in the center of the sky.

JOHN BULL: It's true, he's stopped going around. He's rising straight up. He's halfway between the two hills.

The ball does what he says.

FIRST MAN: He's stopping. You'd think he was stopping.

FIRST WOMAN: Yes, he *is* stopping.

FIRST LADY: He's stopped to have a look around.

The ball has gone from sight, so has he. Or perhaps there is a tiny doll-like figure of BÉRENGER.

SECOND LADY: At the four corners of the earth.

JOURNALIST: He's dominating the earth.

JOSÉPHINE (*half-anxious, half-admiring*): I'd never have thought him capable of this. He really is someone after all. But it's very risky.

SECOND MAN: He's going higher still!

SECOND WOMAN: Higher still!

FIRST MAN: Higher still!

SECOND WOMAN: Higher still!

LITTLE BOY: He's a balloon, he's a balloon.

FIRST LADY: He's giving out distress signals.

JOSÉPHINE: Oh dear! Is he going to fall?

MARTHE: Don't worry. You know very well he said he couldn't fall.

JOURNALIST: He's not losing height, he's not falling.

SECOND LADY: Something's gone wrong.

BÉRENGER, *the little doll, gets bigger.*

FIRST LADY: What's he seen?

JOHN BULL: He doesn't look very pleased.

FIRST LADY: What's he seen?

JOSÉPHINE: What on earth *can* he have seen?

FIRST MAN: What's he seen?

SECOND LADY: He's vanished from sight.

JOSÉPHINE: He's vanished from sight. He's disappeared.

Gradually the stage darkens. Blood-red glimmering

lights and great rumbles of thunder or bombardment. In the silence and half-light that follow, a spotlight picks out and isolates JOSÉPHINE, *lighting her at first dimly.*

JOSÉPHINE: He's got a positive mania for leaving me alone! He takes every opportunity to abandon me. Yet he knows I get frightened. . . . He knows perfectly well. I've no one in the world, nobody, nobody, nobody.

MARTHE (*rather to one side, and more in the shadow than* JOSÉPHINE): You've got Papa.

JOSÉPHINE: I'm alone. I'm quite alone, cast off into the darkness and abandoned.

MARTHE: But look, *Maman,* I'm here.

JOSÉPHINE: I'm all alone in a great big forest, far away from everything. I'm frightened.

The JOURNALIST *and the* SECOND ENGLISHMAN *cross the stage. They are transformed completely enough for us to be astonished at the change, but still recognizable; they look slightly distorted as in a dream. Perhaps the lighting can suggest this change. Or perhaps they could wear masks representing their own faces. This may be the best solution. In any case the lighting can tone down the color of their clothes. They are talking.*

JOURNALIST: You see, friendship . . . friendship was a snare and a delusion. Besides it slowly sucks the life out of you. Loathing is better. It provides the most favorable background for life. It's the only thing can give us strength. Loathing means energy. It's energy itself.

92 / *Eugène Ionesco*

SECOND MAN: So we ought to loathe each other? Can I loathe you and still be polite?

JOURNALIST: It's more relaxing that way. But we've always loathed each other. Friendship was what we used to cover up our weakness, we were too timid and repressed our loathing of one another. Nowadays we're living through an age of science and cerebration. We must take a good look at ourselves, gaze straight in the face of ourselves and the truth. And to get a true perspective we must keep a certain distance apart.... (*As he walks, he knocks into the* SECOND MAN *with his elbow.*) Oh, sorry! I knocked into you. So sorry!

SECOND MAN: It's nothing, really! Please don't apologize!

JOURNALIST: See what I mean?... All this sentimentality in our day and age.... We can't believe in that now, we're not children any more. Friendship's a ludicrous word, hypocritical: now it's gone for good.

SECOND MAN: I think you must be right, old man.

They go out.

MARTHE: I'm here, I tell you. Can't you hear me?

JOSÉPHINE: Nobody.

MARTHE: Don't you want to hear me? *Maman,* I'm here. And there are all the others.

JOSÉPHINE: Yes, yes, I can hear. Don't shout like that!

MARTHE: All the other people.

JOSÉPHINE: What people?

MARTHE: Friends, we've got lots of friends.

JOSÉPHINE: And you call them friends? What am I to them? And what are they to me? No, no, they're not friends. Empty vessels in a desert. Monstrously indifferent, selfish, cruel and enigmatic. Each confined in his own little shell.

MARTHE: Oh!

JOSÉPHINE: No, no, Marthe, not you, of course. But what can you do? You're only a little girl.... What can you do?... And I'm so tiny in this gigantic world of ours. I'm like a frightened little ant that's lost her way, looking for her companions. My father's dead, my mother's dead, all my family are dead. The neighbors who used to know us have left the town where I was born, and scattered all over the world. I've never heard from them since. There's no one left, not a soul in the world.

MARTHE: There's all the rest, all the other people. There are lots of people.

JOSÉPHINE: I don't know them and they don't know me. They're strangers.... Once I had my parents who were big and strong. And they took me by the hand to guide me through life. Nothing frightened *them*. They just marched straight on. With them I had nothing to fear.... In those days I had nothing to fear, nothing to fear.... Except the fear of losing them. All the time I used to think that I would have to lose them. That was inevitable. I knew it, I knew it. And then very quickly that day came, too quickly I'm afraid! It's such a long time, such a long time now since I've been all alone, such a long time since they left me by myself. ... And I've never got used to them not being here. And I never shall. Never, never.... I've been left all alone, and I'm frightened, so frightened. I'm lost and I just wander about.... No one knows me and no one loves me, I mean nothing to other people. For them I don't count. For them I just don't count.

MARTHE: I'm growing up. I'll soon be as strong as your mother was. I'll protect you.

JOSÉPHINE: I fight to protect myself, in my despair, as best I can. Fear has taught me how. The clawing fingers of fear have driven me on. And I fight tooth and nail.

MARTHE: You must love people. If you love them, they won't be strangers to you any more. If you stop being afraid of them, they won't be monsters any more. Deep down in their shells, they're frightened too. Love them. Then hell will exist no more.

MARTHE *is no longer visible. In the semi-darkness a wall can be seen. A terrified child, rather like the little English boy, dashes to the wall and tries to climb it. Without success. A large fat character appears, not unlike* JOHN BULL, *chasing the child. It is in fact* JOHN BULL *and the* LITTLE BOY *also slightly transformed as in a dream.*

FAT MAN: You stinking little brat!

CHILD: Let me go, sir.... I'm sorry, sir.

FAT MAN: Filthy little swine! So you'd get away from us, would you? Trying to escape! Why? Just tell me why?

CHILD: I'm very sorry, sir. I wanted to go for a walk in the light. I wanted lots of sky.

FAT MAN: Greedy child. Hooligan. (*He slaps the boy and pulls the weeping* CHILD *away by his ear.*) You thought I couldn't catch you, did you?...

CHILD: Not the cell, sir, I won't go back to that cell!

FAT MAN: Stupid brat, you've got to learn that the light's a lot more beautiful when it's seen from the bottom of a nice black hole. And a clear blue sky's a lot purer when you look at it through a high barred window.

CHILD: Not the cell, sir, I won't go back to that cell!

FAT MAN (*pulling him off*): We'll teach you. We'll educate you. You'll understand one day ... or you'll learn to put up with it.

They go out. Strange apparitions can be seen, which are then recognizable as the FIRST ENGLISHMAN *and the* FIRST ENGLISHWOMAN, *the* SECOND ENGLISHMAN *and the* JOURNALIST, *slightly transformed, as if somewhat caricatured, and with exaggerated gestures. They go up to* JOSÉPHINE.

JOURNALIST: Oh Madame, Madame, all our hearts are with you.

THE THREE ENGLISHMEN (*together*): All our hearts are with you. All our hearts are with you.

FIRST MAN: If there's anything we can do....

SECOND MAN: We'd do anything for you.

JOSÉPHINE: You're very kind, Madame, Messieurs.

FIRST WOMAN: I know what it's like to be all alone in a foreign country. We've had the same experience. My husband will help you and all our lovers are at your service.

JOSÉPHINE: Oh, you're so kind, you're much too kind.

JOURNALIST: We're entirely at your service.

96 / *Eugène Ionesco*

JOSÉPHINE: Thank you, I'm covered with confusion.

FIRST MAN: What did she say?

SECOND MAN: She said she's covered with confusion. Imagine that? She said she's covered with confusion.

The three ENGLISHMEN *and the* ENGLISHWOMAN *leave the stage, saying:*

FIRST WOMAN: She's covered with confusion, she told you she was covered with confusion?

JOURNALIST: Yes, she said "Thank you, thank you, I'm covered with confusion."

FIRST MAN (*imitating* JOSÉPHINE): Thank you, I'm covered with confusion.

SECOND MAN: The lady's so naive, she's a very stupid Eve.

JOURNALIST: That's why she's covered with confusion. Hee-hee!

THE TWO MEN: Hee-hee!

FIRST WOMAN: You could take advantage of the situation, yes?

JOURNALIST: There's no advantage there, I guess.

Before they go off, they turn toward her for the last time, and laughingly take their farewell, making grotesque gestures and grimaces.

JOSÉPHINE, *who has her back turned to them, does not notice.* JOSÉPHINE *remains alone; she is on the extreme right of the stage.*

JOSÉPHINE (*in a different tone*): And what about him, where's he always off to? What's he doing? *He* could have helped me. He ought to help me. . . . He abandons me, like all the rest, he doesn't think about me. . . . No one thinks about me. . . .

A gigantic character appears in crimson light dressed in a long red robe with a square red cap on his head. The character could be from seven to ten feet tall, and he can be raised up on a platform hidden by his red robe; he is a JUDGE. . . . *He could have an enormous doll's head; he is terrifying, of course, but that need not prevent the audience from laughing. They can laugh and be frightened at the same time, as when the enormous boots of the dead body appear at the end of* Amédée or How to Get Rid of It. *Laughter will not weaken the effect.*

This monumental JUDGE *advances, on rollers, toward* JOSÉPHINE, *until she is quite near, just facing him; to look at him she has to raise her head.*

To the right and left of the JUDGE *there are two* ASSESSORS, *also dressed in red but not nearly so tall; they are in any case seated; only the* JUDGE *remains standing.*

This is a Court of Law, already set up, which is brought forward on rails. They first glide slowly up to JOSÉPHINE *and will later retire in the same way, being drawn backward.*

Just as they arrive in front of JOSÉPHINE, *one of the* ASSESSORS, *fat and purple-faced, is ringing a little bell. The other one has a hood over his head. The platform stops.*

JOSÉPHINE: I haven't done anything wrong, your Honor. . . . Why do I have to appear before you? What am I accused of? I haven't done anything.

MARTHE (*or the voice of* MARTHE): Don't be frightened, *Maman*. It's a vision, it's a nightmare. It's not real. It's only real if you believe in it. It's real if you think it is. It's real if you want it to be. Don't believe it.

JOSÉPHINE: Yes, it is. It's the Judge. I recognize him.

MARTHE: You've never seen him before. He doesn't exist.

JOSÉPHINE: I'm afraid he does. It's the Judge.

MARTHE: I promise you it's a hallucination, it's an image in a dream. . . . Wake up. Wake up and he'll disappear.

JOSÉPHINE: No, no. . . . He's real.

MARTHE: He *isn't* real, my poor little *Maman*, you're dreaming. . . . You're *dreaming*, I tell you, *believe* me. (MARTHE *disappears again*.)

JOSÉPHINE: I've done no harm to anyone, your Honor. . . . Why have you come? What do you want with me?

FIRST ASSESSOR (*ringing his bell*): Silence! It's we who ask the questions and you must answer.

JOSÉPHINE: I've nothing to say. It doesn't matter how much I search my conscience, I've nothing to tell you, I've nothing to hide, I swear I haven't, I don't understand, I don't understand. . . .

The Court is silent.

If everyone's got to be judged, why start with me? Why did you choose *me*, when there are so many others? . . . Why make *me* the scapegoat? . . . I suppose it's because I'm not so well defended as the others. I haven't a lawyer.

The Court is silent.

A Stroll in the Air / 99

My conscience is clear. Is that why I'm vulnerable? I'm not guilty of anything; it's not my fault. I have no faults. Tell the executioner not to kill me, your Honor.

The Court is silent.

What can I possibly have done? What can you hold against me? There's nothing you can hold against me. I've always been a virtuous and faithful wife.... I've done my duty, always. I've never left my post. I've always stayed at my post and been good, and sad and resigned and unhappy.... (*She starts sobbing.*) And unhappy.... Do you want to punish me because I've been unhappy? You want to condemn me for being good? No, it can't be that, can it? No, it really can't be that?... I don't understand you, I don't understand you, your Honor. Punish the wolves, if you like, but *I'm* a lamb.

The JUDGE *points his first finger threateningly at* JOSÉPHINE. *The two* ASSESSORS *shake their heads approvingly. The headshaking of the* ASSESSOR *who wears the hood is more violent and more grotesque.*

They're going to condemn me. They don't believe me. ... No, no, no.

MARTHE: It's not real, don't be frightened, you only see these figures because you're afraid. It's not true, I swear it isn't. Convince yourself it's not true, all this. You're imagining it, you're inventing it....

JOSÉPHINE: I don't want to.... I don't want to.... What have I done? I haven't done any harm. (*She is sobbing.*)

MARTHE (*kissing* JOSÉPHINE): Poor little *Maman,* hide

your head in my arms and you won't see them any more.

JOSÉPHINE: No, no, no, it's impossible. I don't want to.

MARTHE: But of course it's impossible.... Of course it's not real.

The second ASSESSOR *takes off his hood: it is* JOHN BULL.

JOHN BULL: The reasons of the heart are not those of real justice and logic. If justice seems to you unjust, it is because it is impartial.

The Court of Law is pulled backward, slowly and silently, and disappears into the wings on the left.

MARTHE: What did I tell you? It's just a vision. It can't do any harm. Now the wicked judges have all gone.... Calm yourself, mother, calm yourself, my child....

JOHN BULL *appears from the right with a machine gun that makes no noise when he fires it. He is accompanied by the two* ENGLISHMEN *and the* JOURNALIST.

The little English children appear from the left, with their mothers on either side, followed by the UNDERTAKER'S MAN *and the* DOCTOR *who appeared at the start of the play.*

JOHN BULL: It's better to be a few years early than two minutes too late.... Isn't it, Ladies?

FIRST WOMAN: You're right.

SECOND WOMAN: I entirely agree, Mr. John Bull. You're perfectly right, Mr. John Bull.

The SECOND LADY *appears from the left, looking very agitated.*

A Stroll in the Air / 101

SECOND LADY: Don't think I'm afraid, because I'm not. I'm just indignant, terribly indignant.

JOHN BULL (*to the two* ENGLISHMEN *and the* JOURNALIST): Well then, since your wives share your own opinions (*to the* JOURNALIST), and everything's all right . . . let's get on with it.

JOURNALIST: Carry on then.

UNDERTAKER: Carry on then.

FIRST MAN: As it's got to be, you might as well do it.

SECOND MAN: Yes, you might as well do it.

SECOND LADY: I strongly protest. . . .

UNDERTAKER: Better now at that age than later. . . . Now, they won't realize what's happening. Later on, they'd suffer and they'd resist.

JOURNALIST: It's for their own good.

JOHN BULL (*taking aim with his rifle or machine gun*): Ladies, close your eyes.

FIRST WOMAN: Let's close our eyes.

SECOND LADY: I protest.

JOHN BULL (*to the* OLD LADY): Get out of the way. It's too late for you now.

JOHN BULL *takes aim, and fires. The two children fall to the ground.*

SECOND LADY (*who had moved away*): I protest most violently. . . .

JOHN BULL: Ladies, open your eyes.

FIRST WOMAN: Is it over already?

SECOND WOMAN: How quick you are!

UNDERTAKER: It's like a mercy killing. It's not exactly mercy killing, but you could say it's preventive mercy killing.

SECOND LADY: I protest most strongly, most violently.

JOURNALIST (*to* ENGLISHWOMEN): Now you can pick up your children.

UNDERTAKER: It's not worth the trouble, ladies. Leave it to me. That's my job. I'll take charge of it. . . .

SECOND WOMAN: We've only done our duty.

JOHN BULL: And we've done ours. (*To the* DOCTOR:) Doctor, will you verify that these children are well and truly defunct.

SECOND LADY: I protest. It's absolutely disgraceful. It shouldn't be allowed. (*To the* DOCTOR-UNCLE:) You call yourself a doctor, and you accept it all just like that?

DOCTOR-UNCLE: I don't accept it. I'm resigned to it.

JOSÉPHINE: What, is it you, Doctor-Uncle? You're not in this too?

DOCTOR-UNCLE (*to* JOSÉPHINE): This way, you see, I shall avoid being judged myself. . . .

JOHN BULL (*to the* ENGLISHWOMEN, *with a certain gallantry*): Since you have no more children to bring up, I wonder, ladies, if you'd mind . . . taking your turn?

FIRST WOMAN: We don't mind at all.

JOSÉPHINE (*to the* DOCTOR): I'd never have thought you could behave so contemptibly.

A Stroll in the Air / 103

DOCTOR-UNCLE: What do you expect, my poor Joséphine? We all acquire wisdom in time. Besides, it's better that way. In any case it was bound to happen. It's all over much quicker this way. It's better sooner than later, much better to be thirty years early than two seconds too late.

JOSÉPHINE: You, you who've saved so many human lives, thousands of children ...

DOCTOR-UNCLE: This is how I redeem myself.

JOHN BULL (*to the* ENGLISHWOMEN): And your husbands too. Your husbands will follow you. (*To the* ENGLISHMEN:) After you, gentlemen, if you don't mind.

Slight, discreet hesitation on the part of the ENGLISHMEN. *The* ENGLISHWOMEN *advance with* JOHN BULL *behind, holding his machine gun.*

MARTHE (*to* JOSÉPHINE): It's not real, don't get so upset ... none of it is real.

The UNDERTAKER'S MAN *picks up the children, one under each arm. The* OLD LADY, *the children, the* DOCTOR-UNCLE, *the* UNDERTAKER'S MAN, *the* ENGLISHMEN *and* WOMEN, JOHN BULL *and the* JOURNALIST, *all disappear from both sides of the stage.*

The MAN IN WHITE *appears. Same apparatus and installation as for the Court of Law. On the right of the* MAN IN WHITE, *a* HANGMAN *in white with a white hood. To the right of the* HANGMAN, *a gibbet.*

In the background there is a twilight sky with a red sun. As soon as this group approaches JOSÉPHINE, *they stop and remain silent for a few moments.*

JOSÉPHINE: No, no.

MARTHE (*to* JOSÉPHINE): Don't take any notice. All you have to do is not believe in them.

MAN IN WHITE (*indicating the gibbet to* JOSÉPHINE): Madame, wouldn't you like to? Make up your mind.

JOSÉPHINE, in her terror, still keeps up the polite habits of society, and so does the MAN IN WHITE: *nightmare and drawing room manners.*

JOSÉPHINE: No, please don't ask me. I'm terribly sorry, Monsieur. I don't feel like it, I'd really rather not.

MAN IN WHITE: You would, if you took my advice.

MARTHE: She doesn't want to, I tell you. And if she's said she doesn't want to ...

MAN IN WHITE (*to* JOSÉPHINE): Think carefully. You really won't? Take your courage in both hands!

JOSÉPHINE: Oh no, oh no, really, not now.

MAN IN WHITE: In any case, you won't be able to put it off indefinitely.

JOSÉPHINE: No, no. We'll see, perhaps tomorrow. Oh please, no, not now, the day after tomorrow. Not today. I really don't feel like it just now.

MARTHE: You see, she really doesn't feel like it.

HANGMAN (*to* JOSÉPHINE): Madame, why put off till tomorrow what you might just as well do today? Why not get it over?

MARTHE (*to the* HANGMAN): Mind your own business and don't interrupt our conversation. Leave her alone.

JOSÉPHINE: No.

A Stroll in the Air / 105

MAN IN WHITE: You know very well you can't escape. You know very well that everyone goes the same way. You don't gain anything really, only a little time.

JOSÉPHINE: Tomorrow, tomorrow, tomorrow. Give me a little longer, Monsieur Man-in-White. . . . Give me a little longer, Monsieur Hangman.

MAN IN WHITE: If you really insist. But it's a mistake. However, if you really don't want to, we're not in a desperate hurry yet.

HANGMAN: They're all alike, they're so stupid. Just try and get them to see reason. . . . (*To* JOSÉPHINE:) And yet you've just seen for yourself, the English people all agreed. Even the children.

MARTHE: You didn't ask their consent. You didn't ask their consent!

The MAN IN WHITE *makes a sign: gibbet,* HANGMAN, *then the* MAN IN WHITE *himself all slowly disappear to the left.*

You see, *Maman*, it wasn't real. If you don't want it to be, it isn't real. It all depends on you. Now stop having nightmares. Promise me you won't have any more nightmares. . . . No more nightmares. . . . They've gone, they didn't really exist!

JOSÉPHINE: I'm not so sure.

Change in the lighting: the ENGLISHMEN, *the* ENGLISHWOMEN, JOHN BULL *and the* JOURNALIST *reappear as they did at the beginning.*

MARTHE: You see, the little English Children are still here.

The stage gradually darkens. It glows blood red with great sounds of thunder or bombardment.

Light returns to the stage again; but this time it is a different light, which makes the landscape look gray and sad, a kind of twilight; perhaps in the background you could see a few smoking ruins, a cathedral, a smoking volcano. You can also hear:

THE VOICE OF BÉRENGER (*despairing*): I can see, I'm afraid I can see everything! And there's no more hope. It's impossible, it's just impossible. And yet, perhaps, if it were only a dream. No, no it's not a dream. Oh God!

FIRST LADY: He's spinning slowly around.

JOHN BULL: Like a top that's running down.

SECOND LADY: He looks as though he's coming down.

SECOND WOMAN: He *is* coming down.

MARTHE (*to* JOSÉPHINE): You see, he's coming down. He's coming.

JOSÉPHINE: A good thing too. I don't feel quite so anxious.

FIRST WOMAN: He could have stayed up there as long as he liked.

FIRST LADY: *I* wouldn't have come down.

SECOND LADY: But the man's got a family.

FIRST MAN: He's coming closer. You can see him better.

SECOND MAN: He's gesticulating. You'd think he was talking.

FIRST LADY: Though we can't hear him.

JOURNALIST: He's coming down very gently.

A Stroll in the Air / 107

SECOND LADY (*to* JOSÉPHINE): You must be proud of your husband.

MARTHE: He's coming down so sadly. He looks so depressed.

FIRST LADY (*giving the* LITTLE GIRL *a bouquet of flowers*): You must give the Gentleman this bunch of flowers.

JOSÉPHINE (*to* MARTHE): Why do you think he seems sad? He's been very successful.

SECOND LADY (*giving a rather torn and dirty flag to the* LITTLE BOY): And you can march in front of him when he arrives, with this.

JOHN BULL: It's not much of a triumph in my opinion.

MARTHE: Yes, he *is* sad. You can tell that from his movements, from the general look of him.

FIRST MAN: He's coming nearer and nearer.

The sounds heard just now have got gradually fainter. Now there is nothing but the sound of firecrackers, and there is a kind of twilight, red perhaps. You can see a few firecrackers exploding with brief flashes of blood red.

Through the spluttering sound, you can also hear in the distance a kind of Fourteenth of July dance music, derisively triumphant.

FIRST WOMAN: He's coming down step by step.

FIRST LADY: It's as though he was coming down an invisible staircase.

SECOND LADY: There he is. (*To* JOSÉPHINE:) There's your husband, Madame.

SECOND WOMAN: Where can you see him?

FIRST MAN (*pointing with his finger*): There! At the end of my finger.

FIRST WOMAN: He's brushing the top of that tree.

SECOND MAN: He's not in a hurry. He's picking a leaf.

JOURNALIST: Automatically.

The leaf can be seen, fluttering down.

JOHN BULL: Here he is.

SECOND LADY: Bravo, Madame Bérenger!

BÉRENGER reappears, alighting gently on the stage. They all go toward him.

LITTLE GIRL: Bravo, Monsieur Bérenger!

The LITTLE BOY has got a kind of trombone, which he blows into in an effort to play some victory march. He has already given his flag to BÉRENGER who drops it at once. BÉRENGER has not taken the flowers from the LITTLE GIRL either, they too drop on the stage.

Bravo!

JOSÉPHINE: He's quite deflated. (*To* BÉRENGER:) What did you see up there? Are you tired?

The ENGLISHWOMEN wave their colored handkerchiefs and clap their hands, shouting "Hurrah for Bérenger!" The ENGLISHMEN are silent.

It should be pointed out that before his feet touched the grass again, BÉRENGER, in his descent, just grazed the heads of the ENGLISHMEN, who had to move out of the way.

A Stroll in the Air / 109

JOURNALIST: Tell us all your impressions, Monsieur Bérenger.

JOSÉPHINE: I'm so glad you're back. I must say, I was really frightened after all. You ought to have warned me. Tell the Journalist all your impressions.

BÉRENGER: I . . . I . . . (*He falls silent.*)

JOHN BULL: Monsieur, may I ask you how you did it?

FIRST MAN: And what you did?

SECOND LADY: You saw for yourself, he's been flying.

BÉRENGER: I have been flying, yes, I've been flying all right. . . .

FIRST LADY: But you saw for yourself.

JOURNALIST: Why have you been flying?

BÉRENGER: I don't know. . . . I couldn't help myself.

JOHN BULL: What we mean is "Why do you *fly?*" What do you hope to achieve with an exploit like that?

FIRST MAN: It's not true. You weren't really flying at all. We were watching carefully: you were walking over an invisible arch. On something solid.

FIRST WOMAN: Oh, no! There wasn't any arch!

FIRST LADY: There was no invisible arch.

JOURNALIST: There could have been. If the air solidifies, it does make an invisible arch.

SECOND MAN: Anyone could have done that.

SECOND WOMAN (*to her husband*): Don't exaggerate!

FIRST LADY: Why don't you try, then?

SECOND LADY: That's true, you could at least try.

SECOND MAN: Anyone can do the same. Absolutely anyone.

FIRST MAN: All we need is for you to tell us the exact position of that invisible air bridge.

BÉRENGER: There isn't any arch apart from the silver bridge. I was just flying, that's all, I promise I was flying.

JOHN BULL (*to the other English characters*): In any case, there's nothing very extraordinary about his achievement.

SECOND MAN: That's right. A flying kite does exactly the same.

SECOND WOMAN: Well, it's something anyway for a man to be a flying kite.

JOHN BULL: Why give yourself all that trouble when you can reach the other side of the valley in a few seconds by crossing the bridge in a car.

FIRST MAN: Or in one of our planes.

SECOND MAN: Or in one of our rockets.

JOURNALIST: It took him a good five minutes just to cover half the distance.

FIRST LADY (*to* JOSÉPHINE): They're too critical. Don't listen to them, Madame.

SECOND LADY: People are so envious.

JOURNALIST: Five minutes at least, or even six! It's much too long! It's a terrible waste of time.

FIRST MAN: And we haven't any time to waste.

JOHN BULL (*to* BÉRENGER): We're not prepared to patent your system.

JOURNALIST: Anyway, just to keep my professional conscience quiet, I'm going to ask you to give us your impressions.

BÉRENGER: What can I tell you? What on earth can I tell you?

SECOND WOMAN (*to* JOHN BULL): I think we ought to, we ought to patent it.

FIRST MAN: Technology does far better, Madame. Technology does better. It's against all the principles of progress and the development of the human mind to return to natural laws.

MARTHE: Bravo, Papa, bravo, bravo! Oh! But he really does look deflated.

JOSÉPHINE: What's the matter with you?

SECOND MAN (*to the* FIRST WOMAN): I assure you, Madame, it may be a brave thing to do, but it's nothing out of the ordinary. Absolutely any Englishman, with a little training, a little training . . .

JOSÉPHINE: What's the matter with you? You ought to be proud of yourself! What a character! You don't look satisfied, you never look satisfied.

SECOND WOMAN: Defend yourself, Monsieur, explain yourself.

FIRST LADY: Tell them how important this is.

FIRST WOMAN: You have all our admiration.

JOSÉPHINE (*to* BÉRENGER): You see.

JOHN BULL (*to the English characters*): Now listen to me, the whole incident presents no interest at all.

JOURNALIST: Puerile! The only height he's scaled is the height of ridicule.

JOSÉPHINE: Believe me, it *is* a success, there will always be someone to criticize.

SECOND LADY: Anyone who's been as high as you have won't be put off by a little thing like that.

FIRST WOMAN: Say something, Monsieur, say something.

MARTHE: He's frightened, he's tired. His eyes look quite wild....

JOSÉPHINE: Oh God! What a look! What can you have seen on the other side?

FIRST MAN: He can't have seen anything at all, going at such a speed, and with no precision instrument.

FIRST WOMAN: What did you see, Monsieur, on the other side? Tell us. What did you see?

THE ENGLISHWOMEN (*together*): What did you *see?*

BÉRENGER: I saw ... I saw ... some geese....

JOHN BULL: He saw some geese. He's a practical joker.

BÉRENGER: Men with the heads of geese.

JOURNALIST: Is that all? That's not much.

BÉRENGER: Men licking the monkeys' behinds and drinking the sows' piss.

JOURNALIST: Monsieur, Monsieur! Don't be indecent!

JOHN BULL: Little children have delicate ears.

FIRST MAN: What depravity!

JOSÉPHINE: Herbert, watch your language!

On hearing Bérenger's words, the LITTLE BOY *says: "Hear what he said?" And the* LITTLE GIRL *replies: "He said the monkeys' behinds and the sows' piss."*

BÉRENGER: I saw columns of guillotined men, marching along without their heads, columns of guillotined men ... crossing enormous plains. And then, and then, I don't know, giant grasshoppers and fallen angels, and archangels gone astray.

JOHN BULL: He's an old humbug.

JOURNALIST: He hasn't seen anything at all. He simply read that in the Apocalypse.

FIRST WOMAN (*to* LITTLE BOY): No, you *can't* have it. It's not a children's book.

BÉRENGER: I saw whole continents of Paradise all in flames. And all the Blessed were being burned alive.

JOURNALIST: If that's all you've got to tell us, Monsieur, it's not worth taking notes.

SECOND WOMAN: Make an effort, Monsieur Bérenger, just to please *us*. We admire you. Tell us all about your journey.

BÉRENGER: I'm trying to.

FIRST WOMAN: Something more interesting, more up-to-date.

BÉRENGER: I saw some knives, I saw some graves. . . .

FIRST MAN: And he thinks we'll be amazed at that. We've got steelworks and cemeteries all over the place.

JOSÉPHINE: But where else did you go? What else did you see?...

BÉRENGER: In another place, the earth was cracking... the mountains were caving in and there were oceans of blood... of mud and blood and mud....

JOHN BULL: Not much imagination. If that's literature, I don't think much of it.

JOURNALIST: Compare it with *our* poets!

FIRST MAN: And even with *foreign* poets! You don't have to look any further than Dante.

SECOND MAN: There's not much of interest here.

SECOND LADY: And yet, I must say it impresses me, it quite moves me.

MARTHE: But when you went higher up? When you were right in the air?

JOSÉPHINE: What else did you see up there?

BÉRENGER: I went such a long way up. To see what was going on toward the other points of the compass.

JOURNALIST: And when you got there, what did you see?

JOHN BULL: Did you see anything more exciting?

FIRST MAN: Not so vulgar?

SECOND MAN: A bit more cheerful?

BÉRENGER: I reached the ridge of the invisible roof where space and time come together, and I touched it with my head, I gazed to the right, to the left, behind and in front of me.

A Stroll in the Air / 115

While he has been saying the last sentence, the FIRST MAN *has remarked to his wife: "It's getting late for the little one."*

FIRST WOMAN (*taking the child by the hand*): Come along, let's go home.

The FIRST MAN *and the* LITTLE BOY *move away slowly to the left, where the vague cracklings and feeble glimmerings of a fireworks display suggest some gloomy celebration.*

BÉRENGER: Bottomless pits, bombardments, bombardments, bottomless pits opening over the plains, already ravaged and deserted centuries ago.

SECOND MAN (*taking his wife and little daughter by the hand*): We don't want this nonsense to give her a bad impression.

They stroll slowly away on the opposite side, that is to say to the right, watching the celebrations, which are similar to those on the other side.

BÉRENGER: And then, and then, and then ...

JOHN BULL: If he wanted us to believe him, he might have brought a fox back with him or one of his old sows.

JOURNALIST (*to* JOHN BULL): The pub's open. Coming?

They walk slowly to the back of the stage, and then too quietly disappear with all the others, one by one.

FIRST LADY (*to the* SECOND LADY): It's getting very late.

BÉRENGER: ... millions of vanishing universes, millions of exploding stars.

SECOND LADY: I'm cold. Let's have a cup of tea.

The TWO OLD LADIES *also go off quietly and everyone will have disappeared by the end of Bérenger's speech.*

BÉRENGER: And then, and then, infinite wastes of ice instead of unending fire, then the fire and the ice again. Deserts of ice, deserts of fire battling with each other and all coming slowly toward us ... nearer and nearer and nearer.

JOSÉPHINE: You must tell everyone, tell them quickly what you've seen! Listen to what he's saying!

MARTHE: They're not listening.

BÉRENGER: No one would believe me. I was sure no one would believe me ... mud and fire and blood ... tremendous curtains of flames. ...

MARTHE: *I* believe you. *We* believe you.

BÉRENGER: And even if they did believe me, even if they did believe me ...

JOSÉPHINE: Well, what are you waiting for? Take us one under each arm, now you've proved you can do it, and fly us away.

MARTHE: Quickly, fly us away!

BÉRENGER: But where to?

JOSÉPHINE: Fly us away, much further away, far on the other side of Hell.

BÉRENGER: I'm afraid I can't, my darlings. After that, there's nothing.

JOSÉPHINE: What do you mean, nothing?

BÉRENGER: Nothing. After that, there's nothing, nothing but abysmal space ... abysmal space.

The evening falls blood red, the spluttering of firecrackers can be heard, followed by fleeting red glows.

MARTHE: Can you hear? Can you see? I'm frightened.

BÉRENGER: It's nothing, my darlings, not yet. There's nothing yet but the celebrations, it's a kind of English Fourteenth of July.

With lowered heads BÉRENGER, JOSÉPHINE *and* MARTHE *make for the red lights of the town and go out.*

It's nothing, not just yet. It's nothing, not just yet.

MARTHE: Perhaps that's all that's going to happen, just firecrackers.... Perhaps it will all come right in the end.... Perhaps the flames will die down, perhaps the ice will melt, perhaps the depths will rise. Perhaps the ... the gardens ... the gardens ...

They go out.

Frenzy For Two,
Or More

CHARACTERS

HE
SHE
SOLDIER
NEIGHBOR
NEIGHBOR'S WIFE

An ordinary bedroom—chairs, bed, dressing table, rear window, door on the right, door on the left. SHE *is at her dressing table near the right-hand door downstage.* HE *is pacing about the room—not too nervously, but a little just the same—his hands folded behind his back, his eyes fixed on the ceiling, as if he was watching the flies. Sounds can be heard from outside the room, shouting and gunfire. No words are spoken for about sixty seconds: the man walks about, the woman titivates. Both characters are in dressing gowns and slippers. The man's dressing gown is rather dirty, the woman's betrays a desire to please.* HE *is unshaven. They are not young.*

SHE: The life you promised me! And the life you lead me! I left my husband to go with my lover. How romantic! My husband was ten times better. Seducer! *He* didn't contradict me like a stupid fool.

HE: I don't mean to contradict you. But when you say things that aren't true, I can't let it go at that. I've a passion for the truth.

SHE: What truth? I tell you there *is* no difference. That's the truth. There isn't any. A snail or a tortoise, it's just the same thing.

HE: Not at all. They're not the same animal at all.

SHE: Animal yourself. Idiot.

HE: You're the idiot.

SHE: That's an insult, you revolting imbecile, seducer!

HE: You could at least listen, listen, can't you?

SHE: What am I to listen to? For seventeen years I've been listening to you. It's seventeen years since you carried me off from my home and my husband.

HE: But that's beside the point.

SHE: What point?

HE: The point we're arguing about.

SHE: That's over and done with. There's no point going on. A snail or a tortoise, it's the same thing.

HE: No it's not.

SHE: Yes it is.

HE: But anyone will tell you.

SHE: Who's anyone? Doesn't the tortoise have a shell? Answer me that.

HE: So what?

SHE: And doesn't a snail have one too?

HE: Yes. So what?

SHE: And doesn't a snail or a tortoise retire into its shell?

HE: Yes. So what?

SHE: Isn't a tortoise or a snail a slimy animal with a short body that moves very slowly? Isn't it a tiny sort of reptile?

HE: Yes. So what?

Frenzy for Two / 123

SHE: There, you see! I've proved it. Don't people say "Slow as a tortoise" and "Slow as a snail"? And isn't a snail, and by that I mean a tortoise, a creepy-crawly thing?

HE: Not exactly.

SHE: Not exactly what? You mean a snail isn't creepy-crawly?

HE: That's right.

SHE: There, you see! It's the same as a tortoise.

HE: No, it isn't.

SHE: You're so stubborn! Tell me why, slug!

HE: Just because.

SHE: A tortoise, and by that I mean a snail, goes around with a house on its back that is built for itself. That's why it's so slow.

HE: *Slugs* are related to snails. They are homeless snails. Tortoises have nothing to do with slugs. So there, you see! You see, you *are* wrong.

SHE: You tell me why, zoologist, just tell me why I'm wrong.

HE: Well, because . . .

SHE: What's the difference? Tell me, if you can see what it is!

HE: Because. . . . The difference is. . . . But I admit there's some similarity too.

SHE: Then why insist on the difference?

HE: The difference is that . . . that. . . . It's hopeless, because *you* won't admit there's any. Besides, I'm too tired. I've explained it all before, we're not going to start *that* again. I've had enough.

SHE: You won't explain because you're wrong. You can't give reasons for the simple reason that you haven't any. If you were honest, you'd admit it. But you're not, you've never been honest.

HE: You're talking nonsense, absolute nonsense. Now look here, slugs belong to the ... or snails, I mean ... whereas the tortoise ...

SHE: Oh! Shut up! I've had enough! You'd better keep quiet. I can't stand any more of your natter natter.

HE: Neither can I. I can't stand any more from you. I don't want to hear another word.

The noise of a loud explosion.

SHE: You won't have to! We'll never agree.

HE: How can we agree? We'll never get on together. (*Pause.*) Look here, does a tortoise have horns?

SHE: I've never noticed.

HE: Well, a snail does.

SHE: Not always. Only when it shows them. A tortoise is a snail that doesn't. What does a tortoise live on? Lettuce. So does a snail. So it *is* the same animal. Tell me what you eat and I'll tell you who you are. Besides, snails are edible. And so are tortoises, at least when they're turtles.

HE: They're not prepared in the same way.

SHE: And yet they don't eat each other. Neither do dogs. Because they're the same species. It means they're just different examples of the same kind. But they're the same species, the same species.

HE: You belong to a fine species!

SHE: What did you say?

HE: I said *we* don't belong to the same species.

SHE: You should have noticed that long ago.

HE: I noticed it the very first day. By that time it was too late. I should have noticed it before I met you. The day before. The very first day I realized we'd never understand each other.

SHE: You ought to have left me to my husband, to family affection, you should have told me and left me to do my duty. It was a pleasure to do it, every minute of the day and the night.

HE: What on earth made you come with me?

SHE: *You* made me. You *took* me! Seducer! Seventeen years ago! At that age we don't know what we're doing. I left my children behind. The children I never had. But I could have had children. As many as I liked. I could have been blessed with sons and they'd have known how to protect me. Seventeen years!

HE: There'll be another seventeen years to come. The machine will last out another seventeen years.

SHE: And all because you can't see further than your nose. I tell you a slug keeps its little house hidden. So it's a snail after all. And therefore it's a tortoise.

HE: Ah! That's it! A snail is a mollusc, a gastropodous mollusc.

SHE: Mollusc yourself! A mollusc is a soft animal. Like a tortoise. Like a snail. There's no difference. If you frighten a snail, it hides in its shell, just like a tortoise. That proves it's the same animal too.

HE: What the hell! I don't care! After all the years we've been arguing about the tortoise and the snail...

SHE: The tortoise *or* the snail.

HE: Think what you like, I don't want to hear another word. (*Pause.*) After all, *I* left my wife too. Though it's true, I was divorced at the time. It's some consolation to think the same thing's happened to thousands of people before. No one should get divorced. If I'd never married, I'd never have had a divorce. One never knows.

SHE: You're right, one never knows with you. You're capable of anything. And you're capable of nothing.

HE: A life with no future can never be anything but a life with no future. And even then!

SHE: Some people have all the luck: they're the lucky ones. The unlucky ones haven't *any*.

HE: I'm too hot.

SHE: *I* feel cold. It's not the right time to feel hot.

HE: You see, we don't agree. We never do agree. I'll open the window.

SHE: You want me to freeze to death! You want to kill me.

HE: I don't want to kill you, I just want some air.

SHE: You said we should resign ourselves to being asphyxiated.

Frenzy for Two / 127

HE: When did I say that? I *never* said that.

SHE: Oh yes, you did! Last year. Now you even forget what you've said. You contradict yourself.

HE: I don't contradict myself. It depends on the season.

SHE: You! When *you're* cold, you won't let *me* open the window.

HE: That's the worst of you: you feel hot when I feel cold, you feel cold when I feel hot. We never feel hot or cold at the same time.

SHE: We never feel cold or hot at the same time.

HE: No. We never feel hot or cold at the same time.

SHE: That's because you're not like other men.

HE: What, me? I'm not like other men?

SHE: No. I'm afraid you're *not* like other men.

HE: No, I'm glad to say I'm *not* like other men.

Explosion.

SHE: I'm afraid not.

Explosion.

HE: I'm glad to say. (*Explosion.*) An explosion. I'm not like ordinary men, I'm not an idiot, like all the idiots *you've* always known.

Explosion.

SHE: Listen! An explosion.

HE: I'm not a mere nobody! I used to get invited home by princesses, with gowns cut so low you could have seen their navels, if it weren't for the bodices that hide their nudity. I had the ideas of a genius. If I'd written them down, I'd have been quite well known. I could have been a poet.

SHE: You think you're so much cleverer than other people. Once I thought so too, when I was out of my mind. It's not true. I once pretended to believe you. Because you seduced me. But you're just a moron.

HE: Moron yourself!

SHE: Moron! Seducer!

HE: Don't be insulting! And stop calling me seducer! You ought to be ashamed.

SHE: I'm not insulting you. I'm showing you up.

HE: And *I'm* showing *you* up. I'm removing your make-up. Take that! (HE *gives her a hard slap.*)

SHE: Pig! Seducer! Seducer!

HE: You be careful . . . or watch out!

SHE: Don Juan! (SHE *gives him a slap.*) Serve you right!

HE: Shut up! . . . Listen!

The noise outside gets louder: the shouting and gunfire that could be heard vaguely in the distance have got nearer, and now come from beneath the window. HE, *on the point of reacting violently to her insults, suddenly stops, and so does* SHE.

SHE: What are they up to now? Well, open the window, can't you! Have a look!

HE: Just now you said you didn't want it open.

SHE: I give in. You see how good I am.

Frenzy for Two / 129

HE: That's true. The truth for once, you liar! Anyway, you won't be cold any more. Things seem to be hotting up. (HE *goes to open the window and looks out.*)

SHE: What's happening?

HE: Not much. Three people dead.

SHE: Who are they?

HE: Both sides have lost one. And a passer-by. A neutral.

SHE: Don't stay at the window! They'll shoot you.

HE: I'll close it. (HE *closes the window.*) They're clearing off, anyway.

SHE: That means they've gone, then.

HE: Let me look.

SHE: Don't open it! (HE *opens the window.*) Why have they gone away? Tell me! Close the window, can't you! I'm cold. (HE *closes the window.*) Now we're going to stifle.

HE: But you can still just see them, keeping an eye on each other. Their heads are still just poking around the corner at both ends of the street. We can't go for a walk yet. We still can't go out. We'll make our minds up later. Tomorrow.

SHE: Another wonderful chance to put off a decision.

HE: That's how things are.

SHE: And how they'll go on, how they'll go on. When it's not a storm, it's a railway strike, when it's not flu, it's the war. And when it's not the war, it's still the war. Oh! It's all so easy! And what will it be till the end of time? We know what it'll be, when time runs out.

130 / *Eugène Ionesco*

HE: Haven't you finished yet, doing your hair over and over again? You're beautiful enough, you can't make yourself more beautiful than you are.

SHE: You don't like it when my hair's untidy.

HE: This is no time to titivate. You choose the wrong times for everything.

SHE: I'm in advance of my time. I'm making myself beautiful for the fine times to come.

A bullet from the street breaks a windowpane.

SHE AND HE: Oh! See that!

SHE: You're not hurt?

HE: You're not hurt?

SHE: Didn't I tell you to close the shutters!

HE: I'll complain to the landlord. How can he allow such things? And where *is* our landlord? In the street, of course, having fun. Oh, what people!

SHE: Close the shutters, can't you! (HE *closes the shutters. Darkness.*) Well, put the light on! We can't sit here in the dark.

HE: That's because you told me to close the shutters. (HE *gropes for the switch in the dark and bumps against a piece of furniture.*) Ouch! I hurt myself.

SHE: Clumsy.

HE: That's it, shout at me! Where's the doings? It's not easy to find your way around this house. You never know where the landlord's put the switch. It can't move, yet it's always changing places.

Frenzy for Two / 131

SHE *gets up and makes for the switch in the darkness.* SHE *bumps into him.*

SHE: Can't you look where you're going!

HE: Can't *you* look where you're going!

SHE *manages to switch the light on.*

SHE: You've given me a bump on the forehead.

HE: You trod on my toes.

SHE: You did it on purpose.

HE: You did it on purpose.

They both go and sit down on two of the chairs. Pause.

If I'd never seen you, we'd never have met. How would things have turned out then? I might have been a painter. I might have been something else, what would it have been like? Perhaps I'd be traveling now, perhaps I'd be younger.

SHE: Perhaps you'd have died in an asylum. Perhaps we'd have met just the same some other day. Perhaps there can never be a might have been? How can we know?

HE: Perhaps I wouldn't be wondering now if I've any reason to be alive. Or else I'd have had other reasons for being discontented.

SHE: I'd have watched my children grow up. Or I'd have been a film star. I'd be living in a lovely country house surrounded by flowers. I'd have done . . . what would I have done? What would I be now?

HE: I'm off. (HE *fetches his hat and makes for the door. A loud noise is heard.* HE *stops in front of the door.*) Hear that?

SHE: I'm not deaf. What is it?

HE: A hand grenade. They're throwing hand grenades.

SHE: Even if you *had* made up your mind, we could never get through. We're caught between two fires. Whatever made you choose to live in a no man's land between two sectors?

HE: It was you who wanted this house.

SHE: Liar!

HE: Either you've no memory or you do it on purpose. You wanted this flat for the lovely view. You said it would give me new ideas.

SHE: You're making that up. We never had any ideas.

HE: We could hardly foresee.... There was no indication ...

SHE: You see, you admit it. It's *you* who chose this house.

HE: How could I, if I'd never had the idea. It's either one thing or the other.

SHE: We did it, just like that.

Louder noises from outside. Shouts and commotion from the staircase.

They're coming upstairs. See the door's properly shut.

HE: It *is* shut. It won't shut properly.

SHE: Well, shut it anyway.

HE: They're on the landing.

SHE: On ours?

Knocking is heard.

Frenzy for Two / 133

HE: Keep calm, it's not us they're after. They're knocking on the door opposite.

They listen while the racket goes on.

SHE: They're taking our neighbors away.

HE: They're going upstairs to the next floor.

SHE: They're going down the stairs.

HE: No, up the stairs.

SHE: Down the stairs.

HE: No, up the stairs.

SHE: I tell you they're going *down* the stairs.

HE: You always want to have it your own way. I tell you they're going *up* the stairs.

SHE: *Down* the stairs. You can't even recognize sounds now. That's what fear does for you.

HE: Up the stairs or down the stairs, it makes precious little difference. Next time, they'll be coming for us.

SHE: Let's barricade ourselves in. The wardrobe. Push the wardrobe in front of the door. And you say you have ideas!

HE: I never said I had ideas. But one thing's as good as another. . . .

SHE: Come on, then, the wardrobe, push the wardrobe.

They take hold of the wardrobe which is on the left and push it against the door on the right.

It'll make us feel easier in our minds. At least, that'll do something.

HE: Easier! If you call this feeling easy. You don't know what you're saying.

SHE: Of course I don't. One can never feel easy with you about, one's never at ease with you.

HE: And what do I do that makes you feel uneasy?

SHE: You annoy me. Stop annoying me and you'll still annoy me.

HE: I won't say another word or do another thing. I won't do anything either. Or you'll still say it annoys you. I know only too well what goes on in your mind.

SHE: What goes on in my mind?

HE: What goes on in your mind is what goes on in your mind.

SHE: Insinuations. Nasty insinuations.

HE: What's nasty about my insinuations?

SHE: All insinuations are nasty.

HE: To start with, they're not insinuations.

SHE: Oh yes, they *are* insinuations.

HE: No, they're not.

SHE: They are.

HE: They're not.

SHE: Well, what are they if they're not insinuations?

HE: To know whether they're insinuations or not, you've got to know what insinuations are. Give me a definition of insinuation. I insist you define insinuation.

SHE: You see, they *have* gone downstairs. They've taken the people opposite away. They've stopped screaming. What have they done to them?

HE: Cut their throats, I expect.

SHE: What a funny idea! Oh no! It's not funny at all. But why have they cut their throats?

HE: I can hardly go and ask them, can I? It's not quite the moment.

SHE: Perhaps they haven't cut their throats after all. Perhaps they've done something else to them.

Shouting and noise from outside. The walls shake.

HE: Hear that?

SHE: See that?

HE: See that?

SHE: Hear that?

HE: They're setting off mines underground.

SHE: We'll find ourselves in the cellar next.

HE: Or out in the street. You'll catch cold.

SHE: We'd be better off in the cellar. We can find ways of heating that.

HE: We can hide there.

SHE: They'd never think of looking for us there.

HE: Why not?

SHE: It's too far down. It'll never enter their heads that people like us—or even *not* like us—can live like animals deep down in the earth.

HE: They make a thorough search.

SHE: Well, why don't you clear off? I'm not stopping you. Go and get some air. Take the chance and discover another mode of existence. See if it really exists, another existence.

HE: The chance has come at the wrong time. It's raining, it's freezing.

SHE: You always said *I* was the one who felt the cold.

HE: Well, now it's me. I've got cold shivers down my spine. I've a right to get cold shivers down my spine.

SHE: *You've* every right, of course. *I've* not got any. Not even the right to feel hot. Look at the life you've given me. Just look at it. Just look around at the gay life, with all *this*. (SHE *points to the closed shutters and the wardrobe barring the door.*)

HE: What you're saying's just stupid. You can't really accuse me of being responsible for what's happening, for a world gone raving mad.

SHE: I tell you you ought to have seen it coming. Anyway, you ought to have arranged for things to happen when *we* were away. You're bad luck personified.

HE: Right, then. I'm off. My hat.

HE *is about to fetch his hat when a projectile flies through the window and the shutters and falls in the center of the floor.*

SHE: It's the carapace of a tortoise-snail.

HE: Snails don't have a carapace.

SHE: What do they have, then?

HE: I don't know, a shell.

SHE: It's all the same.

HE: Good God! It's a hand grenade.

SHE: A hand grenade! It's going to blow up, stamp out the fuse.

HE: There's no fuse left. Look! It's not exploding.

SHE: Don't waste time. Take shelter!

SHE goes and hides in a corner of the room. HE makes for the grenade.

You'll get killed, you reckless fool.

HE: We can hardly leave it there, in the middle of the room.

(HE *picks up the grenade and throws it through the window. A loud explosion is heard from outside.*)

SHE: You see! It *did* blow up. Perhaps it wouldn't, if you'd left it where it was, there's not enough air inside the house. It explodes in contact with the air. Perhaps you've killed someone. Murderer!

HE: A few more or less, they'll never notice in the state they're in. Anyway, we're out of danger again, for a while.

Loud noise outside.

SHE: Now we'll never keep out the drafts.

HE: You see, it's not enough to close the shutters. We'd better stand the mattress up, let's put the mattress up.

SHE: You should have thought of that before. Even when you *do* have an idea, it always comes too late.

138 / *Eugène Ionesco*

HE: Better late than never.

SHE: Philosopher, idiot, seducer. Hurry up with this mattress. Help me, can't you!

They take the mattress from the bed and stand it against the window.

HE: Now we won't have a mattress to lie on tonight.

SHE: It's all your fault. We haven't even got two mattresses at home. My husband, the man you took me away from, had several. There was no shortage of them about the house.

HE: It was his job to make them. They were other people's mattresses. It wasn't so clever after all.

SHE: You can see how clever it was at times like this.

HE: At other times, it wasn't so very clever. Your house must have looked very funny with mattresses all over the place.

SHE: He wasn't an ordinary mattress maker. He was a connoisseur, an artist. He did it for the love of the thing. And for love of me. What do *you* do for love of me?

HE: For love of you, I vegetate.

SHE: That's not much.

HE: Oh yes, it is.

SHE: It doesn't wear *you* out, anyway. Lazy devil!

More noise. The door on the left collapses. Smoke.

HE: Oh, this is too much! When you close one door, another's bound to open.

SHE: You'll make me ill. I am ill already. I've got heart trouble.

HE: Or fall flat, all by itself.

SHE: I suppose once more you say that's not your fault!

HE: *I'm* not responsible.

SHE: You're never responsible!

HE: It's all in the logical course of things.

SHE: What's logical about them?

HE: Looked at objectively, there's always some logic in the course of events.

SHE: What shall we do about that door? Put it back where it was.

HE *looks through the door opening.*

HE: There's no one at home next door. They must have gone on holiday. They've left their explosives behind.

SHE: I'm thirsty, I'm hungry. Go and see if there's anything.

HE: Perhaps we could go out. The neighbors' door opens on the street at the back, and that's much quieter.

SHE: All you think of is getting away. Wait for me, while I put my hat on.

HE *goes out on the left.*

Where are you going?

HE (*from the wings*): We can't get out. Of course, the wall's had to collapse on the neighbors' landing. A pile of rubble. (HE *comes in.*) We can't get through, we must wait till things quiet down in our street. We'll remove the wardrobe, then we can pass.

SHE: Let me see. (SHE *goes out.*)

HE (*alone*): If only I'd gone before. Three years ago, Last year or even last Saturday. I'd be far away by now, with my wife, after a reconciliation. She's married again. With someone else then. In the mountains. *I've* been sentenced to an unhappy love affair. And I'm guilty too. The punishment fits the crime.

SHE (*returning*): What are you muttering to yourself? Complaining again.

HE: I'm thinking aloud.

SHE: I've found some sausage in their larder. And some beer. The cork's blown out of the bottle. Where can we sit down to eat?

HE: Wherever you like. On the floor. We can use the chair as a table.

SHE: What a topsy-turvy world!

They sit on the floor on either side of the chair. Noises can be heard from outside. Shouts and shooting.

They've gone upstairs. This time they *have* gone upstairs.

HE: Last time you said they'd gone *down*stairs.

SHE: I never said they wouldn't go *up*stairs again.

HE: It's obvious they would.

SHE: What do you expect me to do about it, anyway?

HE: I didn't ask you to do anything.

SHE: Still, I'm glad you let me please myself.

A statuette falls through a hole that has just appeared in the ceiling. It hits the bottle of beer and breaks. So does the bottle.

Oh, my dress! My best dress! My only dress. A famous dress designer proposed to me once.

HE (*picking up the fragments of the statuette*): It's a little reproduction of the Venus of Milo.

SHE: Now I'll have to sweep it all up. And have my dress cleaned. Where can I find a dry cleaner now? They're busy making war on each other. They find it more restful. (*Looking at the fragments of the statuette.*) It's not the Venus of Milo, it's the Statue of Liberty.

HE: Can't you see she's minus an arm?

SHE: It broke off when she fell.

HE: It was broken before.

SHE: What of it? Doesn't prove a thing.

HE: I tell you it's the Venus of Milo.

SHE: No, it isn't.

HE: Yes it is. Look again!

SHE: You see Venuses everywhere. It's the Statue of Liberty.

HE: It's the statue of Beauty. I like beauty. I could have been a sculptor.

SHE: She's beautiful, your beauty.

HE: A beauty's always beautiful. With a few exceptions.

SHE: And I'm the exception. Is that what you mean?

HE: I don't know what I mean.

SHE: You see, you're insulting me.

HE: I'll prove to you that—

SHE (*interrupting*): I've no wish to hear you prove anything. Leave me in peace.

HE: And you leave me in peace. I want to live in peace.

SHE: And *I* want to live in peace, too. But with you! . . .

Another missile comes through the wall and falls on the floor.

You can see it's impossible with you.

HE: Yes, it's impossible to live in peace. But it's beyond our control. It's impossible, objectively.

SHE: I'm sick of your mania for objectivity. You'd better see to that weapon of war, or it'll explode . . . like the last one. . . .

HE: No, it won't. It won't. It's not a hand grenade this time. (HE *touches it with his foot.*)

SHE: Look out, you'll get us both killed, it'll blow the whole room up.

HE: It's a piece from a shell.

SHE: Exactly, ready to fly in pieces.

HE: If it's a piece from a shell, the shell's already in pieces. So it won't do it again.

SHE: You're driveling.

Another missile, which breaks the dressing table mirror.

They've broken the mirror, they've broken the mirror.

HE: So what!

SHE: How am I going to do my hair? I suppose next you'll say I titivate too much.

HE: Eat your sausage instead.

Noises from above. Rubble falls from the ceiling. SHE *and* HE *both hide under the bed. The noises from outside get louder. Machine-gun fire is now mixed with cheering. They are close to each other, underneath the bed and facing the audience.*

SHE: When I was small, I was a child. Other children my own age were small too. Small boys and small girls. We weren't all the same size. There are always smaller ones and bigger ones, fair children, dark children and children that are neither dark nor fair. We learned reading, writing and arithmetic. Subtraction, division, multiplication and addition. Because we went to school. There were some who did their learning at home. There was a lake, not far away. With fish. Fish live in water. They're not like us. We can't, even when we're small. But we ought to. Why don't we?

HE: If I'd learned the technique, I'd be a technician. I'd manufacture things. Complicated things. Very complicated things, more and more complicated things. To simplify life.

SHE: At night, we used to sleep.

HE (*while rubble goes on falling from the ceiling. At the end of the play there will be no ceiling left at all. And no walls either. In their place one will be able to see staircase-like shapes, silhouettes, banners perhaps.*): One rainbow, two rainbows, three rainbows. I used to count them. Even more. I asked myself the question. The question had to be answered. What exactly was the question? There was no knowing. And yet to find the answer, I had to ask the question. . . . That question. How could you find the answer if you never asked the question? So I asked the question anyway. I didn't know what the question was, but I asked myself the question just the same. It was making the best of a bad job. Those who know the questions are the clever ones. . . . One wonders whether the answer depends on the question or the question depends on the answer. But that's another question. No, it's the same one. One rainbow, two rainbows, three rainbows, four . . .

SHE: Load of rubbish!

HE (*listening to the sounds, watching the rubble fall and looking at the missiles. These missiles should be comic or absurd: broken bits of teacups, pipe bowls, dolls' heads, etc. . . .*): Instead of dying on their own, some people get themselves killed. They're too impatient or they like it that way.

SHE: Or else it's to prove it's not true.

HE: Or perhaps because it's easier. It's more fun.

SHE: The real community spirit.

HE: They kill one another.

SHE: They take it in turn. And yet it seems impossible.

HE: I was in the doorway. I was watching.

SHE: There was a wood, too, with trees.

HE: What trees?

SHE: Trees growing. Faster than we were. With leaves. In the autumn the leaves fall.

Invisible missiles are tearing great holes in the wall. Plaster is falling all around them, dropping on the bed.

HE: Ouch!

SHE: What's the matter? It never touched you!

HE: Nor you.

SHE: What's the matter then?

HE: It could have done.

SHE: That's you all over. Always moaning.

HE: You're the one who's always moaning.

SHE: You're a fine one to talk, I must say! You're always scared of what might happen to you. You're always in a panic, not to say in a blue funk. Because you've no proper job. That's what keeps a man alive. Everyone needs one. If there's a war, they leave you out of it.

Loud noise from the stairs.

They're coming back. This time it'll be for us.

HE: I don't panic for nothing.

SHE: You usually do.

HE: Not this time.

SHE: Because you always want to be right.

No more missiles.

HE: It's stopped.

SHE: I expect it's the tea break.

They come out from under the bed and stand up. They look at the floor strewn with missiles and at the ever-widening holes in the wall.

Perhaps we could get out through there? (*Pointing to a hole in the wall.*) Where does it lead to?

HE: It leads to the stairs.

SHE: Leads to what stairs?

HE: It leads to the stairs that lead to the yard.

SHE: To the stairs that lead to what yard?

HE: It leads to the stairs that lead to the yard that leads to the street.

SHE: Leads to what street . . .?

HE: That leads to the street where there's a war on.

SHE: It's a dead end then.

HE: So we'd better stay. Don't put your hat on, it's not worth putting your hat on.

SHE: When you find a way out, it's always a bad one. Why do you consider going out when we can't?

HE: I'd only considered going out if there'd been a *possibility* of our going out.

SHE: Then there's no point considering the possibility of our going out.

HE: I tell you I'm not considering the possibility of our going out. I tell you I'd only have considered it if the possibility had been at all possible.

SHE: I don't need you to give me lessons in logic. There's more logic in me than in you. I've proved it all my life.

HE: There's not so much.

SHE: There's more.

HE: Not so much.

SHE: More, much more.

HE: Shut up!

SHE: You can't shut me up.

HE: Shut up! Listen, do you hear!

Noise and shouts from the staircase and the street.

SHE: What are they doing?

HE: They're coming up, up the stairs, lots of them.

SHE: They're going to put us in prison. They're going to kill me.

HE: We've not done anything.

SHE: We've not done anything.

HE: That's just why.

SHE: We didn't get mixed up in their affairs.

HE: That's just why, I tell you, that's just why.

SHE: If we *had* been mixed up in them, they'd have killed us all the same.

HE: We'd be dead already.

SHE: That's one consolation.

HE: We survived the bombardment anyway. They've stopped bombarding us.

SHE: They're coming upstairs.

HE: They're coming upstairs.

SHE: They're singing as they come.

Through the holes in the wall climbing figures can be seen and heard.

HE: They've stopped fighting each other.

SHE: They're singing songs of victory.

HE: They've won.

SHE: Won what?

HE: I don't know. The battle.

SHE: Who's won?

HE: The ones who didn't lose.

SHE: And the ones who *did* lose?

HE: They haven't won.

SHE: That's clever. Just as I thought.

HE: You've some logic in you after all. Not much, but a little.

SHE: And what are they doing, the ones who haven't won?

HE: Either they're dead or they're weeping.

SHE: Why are they weeping?

HE: Because they're sorry they were wrong. They can see it now.

SHE: Wrong about what?

HE: Wrong not to win.

SHE: And the ones who did win?

HE: They were right.

SHE: And what if neither of them had lost or won?

HE: Stalemate. Both sides bled white.

SHE: And then what happens?

HE: It's a gray world. Everyone's red with fury.

SHE: The danger's passed, in any case. For a while.

HE: You can stop being frightened.

SHE: It's you who can stop being frightened. You were trembling.

HE: Not as much as you.

SHE: I wasn't as frightened as you.

The mattress tumbles down. Banners can be seen through the window. Lights. Firecrackers.

Damn, damn, damn. They're off again. Just when the mattress has fallen down. Let's hide under the bed.

HE: No, they're not. It's the ceremony, the victory celebrations. There's a parade through the streets. I suppose they're enjoying it. One never can tell.

SHE: They're not going to drag us into their parade! They're going to leave us alone. I hope! As soon as there's peace, they never leave anyone alone.

HE: Still, it's more peaceful like this. We're better off. In spite of everything.

SHE: We're not well off. We're in a bad way.

HE: Bad's better than worse.

SHE (*scornfully*): Philosophy! Philosophy! You'll never be cured of that! Experience teaches you nothing at all. You said you wanted to go out. Go, if you want to.

HE: Not at any old time. If I go out now, they'll cause trouble. I'll have to wait till they've gone home. I'd rather have trouble at home. If *you* want to go out, *I'm* not stopping you.

SHE: I can see what *you* want, all right.

HE: What do I want?

SHE: You want to throw me out in the street.

HE: It's you who want to throw *me* out in the street.

SHE (*looking at the damage and the holes in the wall*): You've done it already. We're in the street now.

HE: We are, and yet not quite.

SHE: They're having fun, they're eating and drinking and dancing. They're terrible, they could do anything, they could attack you, a poor woman like me. Just think! Oh no! Not with *anyone*, I'd rather have an idiot, at least an idiot doesn't have intentions.

HE: You used to hold that against me.

SHE: I still do.

Frenzy for Two / 151

HE: What are they up to now? They've gone quiet. It can't last for long. I know them! I know them! It's frightening enough when they've got something in mind, but when there's nothing, then they start looking around, they start looking around. They might dig up anything. God knows what they might invent. At least, when they're fighting, even if they don't know why at the start, they always find some reason. They don't look any further than that—well yes, perhaps they do—but it all goes to serve one purpose, and when it's over, they've got to start all over again. What are they likely to do? What are they going to dig up?

SHE: Find something for them. You can't. You don't want to rack your brains, you're not interested. Why aren't you interested? You say they're looking for new reasons, so give them some.

HE: There's no reason for anything.

SHE: That won't stop them getting excited. They're no good for anything else.

HE: You hear? They've stopped singing. What are they up to?

SHE: What does it matter to us? Apart from the danger, of course. As you say it's no concern of ours, you can stay indoors, your life is here. (SHE *points to the house*.) If you wanted to, but you're incapable of making anything out of it. You've no imagination. My husband was a genius. And I had the rotten idea of taking a lover. So much the worse for me.

HE: At least they're leaving us in peace.

SHE: That's right. Peace has broken out, they've declared

peace. What's to become of us now? What's to become of us now?

Faint sounds from the street.

HE: It was better before after all. We had more time.

SHE: Before what?

HE: Before it all began . . . before it hadn't begun.

SHE: Before who began what?

HE: Before there was anything, before there was something.

SHE: How are we to start repairing the house?

HE: I wonder.

SHE: It's up to you to find a way.

HE: We'll never get hold of a workman now, they'll all celebrating. They're all out having a good time. Just now they were all immobilized by the war, now they're immobilized by the peace, it's all the same. In any case, they're never here.

SHE: That's because they're always everywhere.

The noise gradually fades.

HE: It's not so easy to be nowhere.

SHE: It's getting quieter. You hear, it's getting quieter.

HE: When things stop happening, they happen fast.

The noise stops entirely.

SHE: It's quieted down completely.

HE: That's true. But they're sure to start again, sure to.

SHE: They'll never learn how to behave. What's the good of it?

HE: That's one way to spend one's life.

SHE: Ours is being spent too.

HE: It's not so stupid the way they spend theirs. But I suppose they're stupid in other ways. There are lots of ways of being stupid.

SHE: You're never satisfied with yours. Always jealous of other people. We've got to repair the house anyway. We can't stay like this. You wouldn't mind if *he* was here now, my husband the mattress maker!

SOLDIER's *head appears through one of the holes in the wall.*

SOLDIER: Is Jeannette here?

HE: Which Jeannette?

SHE: There's no Jeannette here. There isn't a Jeannette.

The two NEIGHBORS *can be seen through the door on the left, which had collapsed.*

NEIGHBOR: We've just arrived. What a surprise! Have you been here all the time?

NEIGHBOR'S WIFE: It must have been exciting.

NEIGHBOR: We were on holiday, we didn't know. But we enjoyed ourselves, where we were.

NEIGHBOR'S WIFE: We're not hard to please. We can enjoy ourselves anywhere, so long as there's a battle.

SHE: Get your door repaired!

HE (*to the* SOLDIER): There's no Jeannette here, no, there's no Jeannette here.

SOLDIER: Where can she have got to? She was meant to wait for me.

HE (*to the* SOLDIER): It's no business of mine, you must mind your *own* business.

SOLDIER: It's on my mind.

SHE (*to* HIM): We must repair the damage. Give me a hand! You can go out after.

HE: You can go out after.

HE AND SHE (*together*): We can go out after.

SHE (*to* HIM): Put the mattress back against the window! Make sure it's firm!

HE: Why? There's no danger now.

SHE: There are drafts. There's flu and there are germs. We must take precautions.

SOLDIER: You don't know who could have seen her?

SHE *pushes the bed in front of the hole through which the* SOLDIER *could be seen, then they put back the door to shut out the* NEIGHBORS. *The sound of a saw can be heard from above.*

SHE: You hear, you see, it's starting again. I told you it would. You contradicted me. But I was right.

HE: Oh no, you're not.

Frenzy for Two / 155

SHE: You mean to say you didn't contradict me? Prove it!

HE: I'm not starting that again.

Headless bodies and bodiless dolls' heads can be seen slowly descending, hanging down from above.

SHE: What on earth's that? (*Her head is brushed by the feet of one of the bodies and* SHE *takes flight.*) Ow! (SHE *goes and touches one of the heads and looks at the others.*) What pretty dollies! Tell me what they are, can't you! Say something! You're usually so talkative. Now you're speechless. What is it?

HE: You're not blind. Headless bodies and over there bodiless heads.

SHE: I was blind when I saw you! I never had a proper look. When I see you now, I wish I was still.

HE: So do I. When I see you, I wish *I* was blind.

SHE: Well, if you're *not* blind, or a complete idiot, just you tell me . . . Ow! They're hanging down like stalactites. Why? You see, the battle's still on.

HE: No. They're dealing out justice in peace and quiet. They've set the guillotine up on the floor above. You can see it's peacetime.

SHE: What are we going to do? You've got me into a fine fix!

HE: Who cares! . . . We'd better hide.

SHE: Give me a hand. Lazy devil! Seducer!

They block the window with the mattress and stop up the doors, while through the ruined walls of the room you can see figures and brass bands passing.

HE: Tortoise!

SHE: Slug!

They slap each other's faces and without pausing set to work again.